DIGITAL
SINGULARITY

DIGITAL
SINGULARITY
A CASE FOR HUMANITY

KEVIN S. PARIKH

with Edward Wilson-Smythe, Whitney Leets, & Sunghea Khil

All proceeds of this book will be contributed to the Avasant Foundation for its Youth Education and Job Creation program.

Printed in the United States of America

Library of Congress Control Number: 2018933952

ISBN Paperback: 978-1-947368-55-2
ISBN Hardcover: 978-1-947368-83-5
ISBN eBook: 978-1-947368-56-9

For my wife, Nita, my children, Karina and Aleena, my family, and all the hardworking, dedicated employees at this great company, Avasant, who provided the vision and inspiration to write this book.

CONTENTS

PREFACE

Imagine a world where technology is all around us, but there is a not a device in sight. It is not interfering in our daily lives—instead, it is automatically supporting us, our relationships, and our businesses. It may have faded into the background, but it is "smarter" than ever, anticipating our wants and needs, acting on our behalf based on our preferences. A digital assistant keeps our identity, relationships, personal data, and our entire financial portfolio secure from hackers while working to make our business and personal connections strong and healthy. It conducts daily transactions for us at lightning speed and in a completely automated fashion. Time-consuming tasks, such as balancing our checkbooks, paying our bills, and buying groceries are no longer a burden.

This is how we will be living not too far from now when we enter *Digital Singularity*, the point at which human experience meets technological omnipresence. Despite the alarmist views espoused by some futurists, *Singularity* will be a time of great opportunity for humanity. It will free us from the mundane and give us more time to dream and innovate—but it will also be a time of great change for business, requiring new strategies, investments, and perspectives for companies that want to not only remain relevant but stay competitive.

Digital Singularity: A Case for Humanity provides a peek into this new digital world. It is a glimpse into not just how we are working today but how we will collaborate, communicate, interact, and innovate in the years ahead. It offers guidance on how to make the journey, for our businesses as well as our personal and professional lives. This book is an acknowledgement that we are moving into a new Digital Age (also known as Digital Singularity), and that both businesses and individuals will need to adapt to this new period of human development.

This book presents unique insights into the emerging technologies that are creating new business and social imperatives for those operating in our increasingly global economy. It explores the requirements needed in our new digital ecosystem, and the future of successful businesses within it, to help companies and executives adapt, thrive, and target the right audiences moving forward. Today we see the potential for human innovation growing exponentially as almost everyone has access to unlimited information via the internet and simultaneous access to any person via global social platforms. As people learn to work without boundaries or limitations, a new reality for business is emerging. The birth of the digital economy is one based on the sharing of information and the power of the *individual*. In this new model there are no barriers. Anyone can interact directly with a CEO or even a head of state. The world is truly flat in this new paradigm.

For twenty years, I have guided professionals in making decisions for their businesses and careers to help them adapt to the changing marketplace and global culture. In *Digital Singularity,* we share our learnings with the goal of providing readers with a new direction that allows them to keep pace with the extraordinary technological and social advancements coming our way.

Thank you,
Kevin S. Parikh

CHAPTER ONE

HOW TECHNOLOGICAL DISRUPTION CHANGES THE HUMAN CONDITION

To understand humanity, we must first understand innovation. Unlike other species, humankind uniquely continues to innovate by creating new technologies and solutions to support its existence. Looking back at the past ten thousand years of humanity, moving from the Stone Age through the Industrial, Information, and Digital Ages, we can see that the transition to each new age has been triggered by the introduction of revolutionary and disruptive technologies. This disruption usually precipitates an immediate impact on labor—often a sudden drop in employment.

As with all such changes, humanity has proven itself to be adaptable and found ways to improve its condition. But the digital disruption we are experiencing now seems to be unfolding faster than earlier revolutions. The emergence of the digital economy is not simply causing job losses; it is also permanently eliminating historic labor categories, resulting in both underemployment and unemployment. Still, as they say, "Necessity is the mother of invention," and we believe that the silver lining to joblessness is the gift of more time to innovate and identify new opportunities.

Consider the impact of the plow on early man. The introduction of this relatively simple tool replaced the labor of many people who cultivated the land. But with fewer people required to tend the fields, there was time to contemplate, imagine, and innovate again. This has been humankind's story from the beginning. New technologies have continually altered the general flow of labor, causing short-term fear and unease for many about their futures. During the Industrial Age, the conveyer belt and mass production further displaced labor with streamlined manufacturing. Again, we witnessed sudden joblessness, underemployment, and despair. But this upheaval prompted a new breed of visionaries, a process that has recurred throughout history. These special people can foresee the disruption, proactively identify opportunities to redirect labor markets, and surf the wave of change.

Recently, as the economy began to recover from the Credit Crisis of 2007–2008, we all became familiar with the paradox of what many economists saw as a "jobless recovery." Simply put, we experienced a growth in economic activity and an unemployment rate that remained stubbornly high. "History tells us that job growth always lags behind economic growth," former president Obama said in 2009, during the nation's financial turmoil and housing crisis. This is yet another example of the natural cycle of innovation, disruption, and recovery.

Today, as we enter the Digital Age, we again encounter an opportunity for people to reinvent themselves in the face of uncertainty and technology-driven disruption. These changes should not be feared but, rather, embraced as an opportunity to innovate, dream, and discover new ways to advance humanity.

Direct from the Assembly Line to the Home

One of the hallmarks of the Industrial Age was the mass production of the automobile. This certainly marked the end of the entire horse-drawn carriage market, as well as the thriving industry for saddle makers and those who managed stables. In the early 1900s, most municipalities maintained stables of horses used for public works and law enforcement. Government employees cared for these animals and ensured their availability for the city. When automobiles began to replace horses, those workers were almost immediately left without

3

work. This included many blacksmiths, carriage, and wagon company workers, and craftsmen who fixed wooden wheels. An entire supply chain was disrupted, and many individuals lost their livelihoods almost overnight. They became the victims of the automobile and its disruptive innovation. For many, it must have seemed like the end of the world. But this innovation generated new jobs and opportunities.

For example, when the Ford Motor Company introduced the Model T, the first mass-produced, mass-marketed car, it is rumored that Henry Ford said, "If I had asked people what they wanted, they would have said faster horses." As humans, we may find it challenging to see what is coming, and we may think our very way of life is over, but it is important to recognize one key ideal: any new, groundbreaking innovation triggers unavoidable shifts in business and culture, but they always spawn new jobs, companies, industries, and business verticals.

Since its invention, the automobile has transformed transportation and permitted global commerce at a level never before experienced in the history of man. Even the efficient but basic technology of the Model T changed the relationships in our personal and professional lives. It united families by reducing the distance between them, and it helped to change working conditions. People could live farther away from the factories and companies where they worked.

And now, with the emergence of the electric vehicle, the cycle of disruption and innovation begins again. Many fear that this new form of clean transportation will disrupt oil markets, parts companies, and the entire supply chain surrounding the internal combustion engine. Surely, many jobs will be lost, but they will hopefully understand that this new technology will drive new opportunities and, ultimately, employment.

Tesla is helping drive this cycle of change. The company's innovation in electric lithium-ion batteries—and the vehicles and drivetrains they power—is beginning to affect the aforementioned oil and gas industry. Some in the financial arena are predicting a looming gasoline crisis in the 2020s as demand for fuel falls off with the proliferation of electric vehicles and technology driving down the price of batteries. By 2040, long-range electric cars could have a sticker price of less than $22,000 (today's dollars), according to a Bloomberg analysis.[1] This move away from a gasoline-dependent economy and society could be the catalyst for the loss of jobs and industries that support cars with more conventional engines.

Tesla's new direct-to-customer sales system is also changing the way we buy cars, which may, eventually, render the

1 Tom Randall, "Here's How Electric Cars Will Cause the Next Oil Crisis," Bloomberg, February 25, 2016, https://www.bloomberg.com/features/2016-ev-oil-crisis/.

deep-rooted dealership distribution system obsolete. If you want to buy one of its automobiles right now, you just go to the company's website, visit its "Design Studio," pick your car, and choose your options, color, and battery range. Tesla sends your car directly to your home. There are no dealerships, no haggling with salespeople, and no reliance on the traditional supply chain.

But despite so much innovation in the car industry, at this time, many people are choosing not to purchase a vehicle at all. With the rise of ride-sharing and subscription-based transportation options, many are simply opting out of owning an automobile. This is especially prevalent among urban dwellers, and is further accelerating the demise of the internal combustion engine and the entire supply chain supporting gasoline-powered vehicles. In fact, how we even think about the automobile is radically changing as well. That is producing a major pattern shift from nearly a hundred years of buying vehicles for the majority of our transportation needs. The cycle of disruption and innovation continues.

There is a new way of doing business in the wake of this technology shift. Today, we are not interested in traveling anywhere to buy our goods and services. Rather, we would prefer them to be delivered directly to our homes. This new model is supporting individualized and highly customized products. Gone are the days when consumers had limited choices or the need to adjust to the design and function of a certain product or service. Now, customers define what they want, how they want it, and when they want it—and companies are responding by manufacturing to customers' exact specifications and requirements.

If you would like a new wardrobe, but perhaps are not following the latest style trends, you no longer have to wait for a clothing company to design a shirt, market it, and attractively display it in a store near you. Instead, you head to the websites and apps for Trendy Butler, Stitch Fix, Nordstrom, and others to create a style profile. A stylist then chooses clothes customized to your needs, fit, and subscription rate. Everything is sent to your house, and you keep what you want. The product is created specifically for the individual consumer, and it evolves over time to reflect an individual's preferences.

The Pace of Change

While recent innovation is propelling us into a new age, it is also clear that this change is happening faster than we ever could have imagined. The pace of technological innovation is accelerating exponentially. Epochs were initially measured in thousands of years. As human civilization developed, centuries, rather than millennia, became appropriate for measuring each era. Today, eras are defined by decades. The shift we have seen in just the past twenty years of human development has been more dramatic than any previous change.

The rate of technology adoption has been racing ahead as well. It took forty-six years, to 1843, for electricity to be used by one-quarter of the U.S. population. The telephone, radio, and television needed thirty-five, thirty-one, and twenty-six years, respectively, to reach that milestone. The PC? Just sixteen years. The mobile phone reached a quarter of the population within thirteen years; the World Wide Web did so in just seven years.[2]

If you can believe it, Apple's iPhone debuted just over one decade ago, in 2007.[3] Ten years later, the smartphone has become so ubiquitous and pervasive it seems like it has always existed. This technology has connected us with long-lost friends and family members. We have become quite adept at texting and taking selfies. We have watched TV shows and movies and listened to gigabytes worth of music. And we have learned to work from anywhere in the world, in any time zone. This technology has changed our lives and how we relate to one

2 Drew DeSilver, "Chart of the Week: The Ever-Accelerating Rate of Technology Adoption," Pew Research Center, March 14, 2014, www.pewresearch.org/fact-tank/2014/03/14/chart-of-the-week-the-ever-accelerating-rate-of-technology-adoption/.
3 BBC News, "Apple's 'Magical' iPhone Unveiled," January 9, 2007, http://news.bbc.co.uk/2/hi/technology/6246063.stm.

another minute to minute. It has propelled us into a "mobile-everywhere" culture and society of technological omnipresence, where tech is all around us. But more importantly, it has created a platform for innovation and possibilities for limitless applications of this technology.

For example, the smartphone has launched a range of jobs, companies, and industries in a relatively short time to make millions of apps, faster mobile phone chips and better batteries, and many other inventions.

With that in mind, think back another ten years: Google had not been founded yet, Amazon was the self-proclaimed "world's largest bookstore," there was no Uber, and the internet was just getting adopted by mainstream users on slow dial-up connections. Many of us accessed the web for the first time via free CD-ROM discs from AOL that arrived in the mail nearly every day.

We Have Hope

While our relationship with technology is changing, it is now simultaneously creating a degree of uncertainty. As we are seeing, with every technological revolution or evolution, some positions and companies will become obsolete as new jobs and industries arise. And as we approach the age of *Digital Singularity*, the point at which human experience meets technological omnipresence, we will experience significant job disruption, accompanied by fear as well as a refusal by some groups to accept what is coming down the pike. Whole industries may disappear due to advances in automation, robotics, and artificial intelligence. And this is of concern to many, a recent survey by Pew Research found. More than twice as many U.S. adults expressed worry rather than enthusiasm (72 vs. 33 percent) about a future where computers and robots might be proficient doing many jobs now performed by humans. But that anxiety was also tempered with some optimism about the many new opportunities on the horizon.[4]

What is unique about this era of technological change, however, is that it is disrupting not only those at the bottom of the economic pyramid. During technology advances of the past, the people at the top of the hierarchy were largely protected. This time around, that is not the case: those at the pinnacle of society, who once initiated the change, are now feeling the impact as much as everyone else.

Some prominent publications may be pumping the brakes, saying, "Who is afraid of disruption?" since a number of long-standing corporations are still seeing profits and high

4 Aaron Smith and Monica Anderson, "Automation in Everyday Life," Pew Research Center, October 14, 2017, http://news.bbc.co.uk/2/hi/technology/6246063.stm.

valuations.[5] But the future is already appearing before us as we head toward Singularity. Digital innovation is causing more traditional companies to take serious hits: More than nineteen brick-and-mortar retail chains have shut down much of their operations since 2014.[6] Toys "R" Us has declared bankruptcy, Barnes & Noble's profits have plummeted, and Whole Foods, recently acquired by e-commerce and distribution juggernaut Amazon, is reportedly dropping prices across the board, making some in retail anxious about their ability to compete. Amazon also recently unveiled that it is testing a plan in some U.S. cities to deliver food items and other goods from Whole Foods stores directly to customers' homes in just two hours, which could help it grab an even larger percentage of the grocery market pie. Even master investor Warren Buffett signaled his perspective by selling off his company's position in Wal-Mart, which Berkshire Hathaway had held for ten years.

Despite the doom and gloom being expressed, we still have a lot to hope for. While technology has clearly purged

5 "Who's Afraid of Disruption," *The Economist*, September 30, 2017, https://www.economist.com/news/business/21729769-business-world-obsessed-digital-disruption-it-has-had-little-impact.
6 Jessica DeNapoli and Tracy Rucinski, "Bankrupt U.S. Retailers Begin to Catch a Break," Reuters, October 6, 2017, https://www.reuters.com/article/us-retail-bankruptcies-analysis/bankrupt-u-s-retailers-begin-to-catch-a-break-idUSKBN1CB0DF.

many jobs and will continue to do so, specifically in agriculture and manual labor, job growth is expected to continue through 2026 in knowledge-intensive sectors, such as professional services and healthcare, according to a U.S. Bureau of Labor Statistics forecast.[7] For the foreseeable future, the jobs less vulnerable to automation and artificial intelligence include those related to managing and developing people and that require expertise in decision-making, planning, and creative work.[8]

President Obama addressed this issue of machines taking over repetitive, labor-intensive, and dangerous tasks in his final address as president, just over seven years after the housing crisis was in full swing. "The next wave of economic dislocations won't come from overseas," he said. "It will come from the relentless pace of automation that makes a lot of good, middle-class jobs obsolete."[9]

---

7 Bureau of Labor Statistics, "Employment Projections—2016-26," October 24, 2017, https://www.bls.gov/news.release/pdf/ecopro.pdf.

8 Michael Chui, James Manyika, and Mehdi Miremadi, "Where Machines Could Replace Humans—and Where They Can't (Yet)," McKinsey & Company, July 2016, https://www.mckinsey.com/business-functions/digital-mckinsey/our-insights/where-machines-could-replace-humans-and-where-they-cant-yet.

9 Claire Cain Miller, "A Darker Theme in Obama's Farewell: Automation Can Divide Us," *New York Times,* January 12, 2017, https://www.nytimes.com/2017/01/12/upshot/in-obamas-farewell-a-warning-on-automations-perils.html.

Do Not "Just Say No"

The fundamental problem that we face is not the change itself, or even the pace of change. It is *resistance* to change. There has been a willful blindness among many who are choosing to ignore the rapid technological shift that is occurring or deny the impact it will have. Some are hoping that, somehow, some way, everything will stay exactly as it has been, because that is the world they have always known—the world they have mastered and feel a certain level of comfort in. But changes are happening too quickly, and many may believe they cannot keep up.

The situation we are facing today is not generational, even though there could be much finger-pointing as we move forward, especially as the Digital Age continues to cause apprehension among certain age groups. The people who will likely best adapt to this new digital environment will be Generation Xers, millennials, and Generation Zers, whose careers have been built around these kinds of disruptive shifts. While millennials may be reacting more enthusiastically to the changes around them that are affecting their jobs—they are now operating in a different economic reality—our shifting relationship with technology is not limited to one group. It will affect all of us.

Some baby boomers may feel under attack with all the rapid change occurring now, but many boardroom executives and forward-thinking boomers will seize upon the opportunity and use it as a basis for transforming their companies toward an individual demand–driven economy.

The solution is to *choose* to stay relevant. If you do not keep up, you are not going to thrive in this new economy, and this remains a frightening prospect for people and companies that have built their entire businesses on a different relationship with technology. A central challenge that we now face is how we will align human capital with emerging digital value chains. We may need to adopt a willingness to retrain, or change jobs, or even transform an industry, but those who are committed to staying relevant will surely sail through the coming sea change.

You have everything to gain by embracing this new era. To be sure, the cost of not adapting is steep. Just fifteen years ago, the Fortune 500 looked much different than it does today—even companies in the top ten have changed. Corporations that once made headlines, like Shell and Exxon, have gradually slipped from importance in the news cycle. Instead, names like Google, Amazon, and Facebook are on the tips of our tongues each day. Even as you read this, new companies you have never heard of are blinking into existence, and within a handful of years, they will change the way we live. Meanwhile, older businesses that rely on timeworn ways of thinking and "legacy" technologies will continue to vanish. One thing that is clear is the cost of not adapting to our digital world: *irrelevance.*

A Way Forward

As the underlying technologies driving this change are defined, we will explain how both individuals and businesses must adapt to benefit from the digital economy. In the digital world, we can demand specially customized products and services. With this new reality, even B2B companies must learn to communicate like B2C companies. All must reconfigure to communicate directly with the *individual*. For example, even a logging company (with no individual customers) must be environmentally friendly, work in a sustainable manner, and maintain a digital voice. All organizations must learn to communicate to the individual.

Over the years we have served the Fortune 500 and have negotiated more than $100 billion in technology deals for our clients. We have advised on deals and built the frameworks for global corporations to adopt and integrate next generation technologies. From this journey we have had a front seat to the change before us. And with this knowledge, we hope to guide you through this revolutionary change. We will offer tips, suggestions, and a new direction designed to aid in the journey to Digital Singularity.

CHAPTER TWO

CORE ELEMENTS OF THE DIGITAL ECONOMY

The rapid rate of change we have witnessed in the last two decades alone has truly been remarkable—not only the underlying technological innovation, but the pace at which the innovation has occurred. The revolutions in processes that have historically evolved over centuries are now happening in just ten or twenty years. Keep in mind that just over three decades ago, less than 10 percent of the population even owned a computer.[1]

Klaus Schwab, the founder and executive chairman of the World Economic Forum, says we are entering a period known

---

1 U.S. Department of Commerce, "Home Computers and Internet Use in the United States: 2000," https://www.census.gov/prod/2001pubs/p23-207.pdf.

as the "Fourth Industrial Revolution," which throughout this book we refer to as Digital Singularity. Soon technology will pull together the physical, digital, and biological worlds in a way that was impossible in past revolutions.[2]

For companies to succeed in this new era, they need to start investing in the technologies that fuel innovation. This is no different than many of the ages we have discussed so far. We refer to these essential requirements as *Technology Prerequisites*.

For example, the Technology Prerequisites for the Information Age were mobile phones, personal computers, tablets, email, global networks, and the World Wide Web. Without your smartphone, could you imagine doing business, taking pictures, connecting with friends, or even buying your groceries? Few of us can remember what life was like before this technology. The prerequisites for Digital Singularity are as follows:

- **Cloud**: An information technology platform delivering computing services, such as storage, networking, and servers, over the internet.

- **IoT**: "The Internet of Things" is the network of "smart" devices, machines, and physical objects that have embedded technologies (such as sensors, below) that

---

2 World Economic Forum, "The Fourth Industrial Revolution, by Klaus Schwab," https://www.weforum.org/about/the-fourth-industrial-revolution-by-klaus-schwab.

Humanity's Relationship with Technology through the Ages

Human Ages	Technology Prerequisites	Pillars of the Age	Rules of the Economy
Digital Singularity (Digital Age)	• Cloud • IoT • Sensors • Artificial Intelligence • RPA • Blockchain • Cyber Security • 3D Printing	• Hyper-Convergence • Digital Moments • Augmented Reality • Digital Twins	• Barrier-free Access • Democratized • Egalitarianism • The Sharing Economy • Transboundary • Communities
Information Age	• Mobile Phones • PCs and Tablets • Email • Global Networks • World Wide Web	• Data Storage • Business & Personal Applications • High Bandwidth Networks	• Electronic transactions • Equal access to information • Social Media • Real time communications
Industrial Age	• Radio, telegraph and television • Centralized Electric Power and Utilities • Fossil Fuel and Steam Engines • Rail, Car, Ship and Airplane transportation	• Global Broadcasting • Mass Production and Machine Automation • Transportation Advances	• Access to electric power • Access to running water • Birth of modern medicine • Global Economy is born
Pre-Industrial Age	• Fire • Wheel • Early Tools	• Agriculture • Hunting	• Trading persists over currency • Subsistence level of living

Singularity | Symbiosis | Master/Slave

allow them to connect to the internet and interact with their physical surroundings and other IoT objects.

- **Sensors**: Technology that detects environmental conditions and sends the information for further analysis or storage. Sensors collect sights, sounds, smells, vibrations, and other perceivable data. This may include radiation sensors or even sensors that examine a visual spectrum beyond the normal human capacity. These technologies collect data that can be analyzed and applied.

- **Artificial intelligence**: This is the simulation of intelligent human behavior by machines, but it is not *intelligence*. By definition, it is "artificial" and lacks sentience.

- **RPA**: Robotic Process Automation is the use of software, aided by AI, that handles high-volume, repeatable tasks previously done by humans.

- **Blockchain**: A digital ledger shared across a network of computers, without the need for a central authority, that securely records and allows transactions to be made using cryptography.

- **Cybersecurity**: The technologies and practices that protect networks, devices, and data against unauthorized access or attacks.

- **3D Printing**: A localized manufacturing device that can use any material (e.g., metal, plastic, clay) to produce solid physical objects from a three-dimensional digital model.

As in any age, the adoption and combination of the Technology Prerequisites lead to new innovations that we have not seen before. These new innovations—*Technology Pillars*—help support and shape the structure and *Rules of the New Economy*. These prerequisites form the outer ring of our "Core Elements of the Digital Economy."

Master/Slave Relationship, Symbiosis, and Singularity

Throughout the ages, the way we have related to technology has changed. These changes can be defined in three distinct relationships: 1) the master-slave relationship, 2) the symbiotic relationship, and 3) the Singularity relationship, which represents the future role of technology and is the focus of this book.

If we look back to humanity's first experience with technology, it can be characterized as a "master-slave" relationship. Our connection with technology was a one-way relationship: We had a device or tool—like an axe, knife, or a typewriter—that we directed, owned, and controlled. The device made our lives easier, but in itself, provided no other benefit. It gave us little insight into our work or ways to make our job easier.

Core Elements of the Digital Economy

- Technology Prerequisites
- Four Pillars of Digital Singularity
- Rules of the New Economy

A transaction within a transaction

A real-time virtual model of your physical self

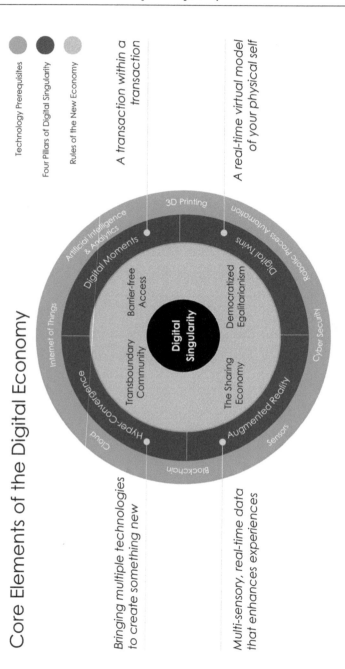

Digital Singularity

Barrier-free Access

Transboundary Community

Democratized Egalitarianism

The Sharing Economy

Digital Moments

3D Printing

Artificial Intelligence & Analytics

Robotic Process Automation

Digital Twins

Internet of Things

Cyber Security

Hyper-Convergence

Augmented Reality

Cloud

Sensors

Blockchain

Bringing multiple technologies to create something new

Multi-sensory, real-time data that enhances experiences

These function-based technologies had only one purpose: to speed up tasks.

In the modern Information Age, we have moved into what is called "symbiosis," where technology, still a physical object, becomes an extension of who we are. Examples include cell phones, pagers, and even audio recording devices. We have a very close relationship with these devices, and we benefit from them as they provide a direct extension of our ability to communicate and connect with the world. They "live" on us and we carry them everywhere. With these devices we can work in real time and more collaboratively with others. Distance has grown shorter with these technologies, and time has grown faster. More can be accomplished in a twenty-four-hour day than ever before in human history.

As we enter the Digital Age, we are seeing the expansion of this technology into mobility, social media, marketing, and product development, such as wearables, intelligent automation, and recent advancements in artificial intelligence. Technology is giving us the power to extend not only ourselves but our connection with the world.

In Digital Singularity, we will be integrated with technology, almost like a single entity. We will experience technology in complete harmony with our normal human activity. This is the point where human experience meets technological omnipresence. Here, the technology is all around us, and it is always on, always listening, always monitoring, and ready to follow our command. (We are not necessarily talking about *cybernetics*, which delves into the communication and control processes in biological and artificial systems, or some type of physical integration with technology.)

This phase, which extends from today through the Digital Age, is crucial because it is where technology fundamentally is changing the nature of how we live. It will be a period of technological ubiquity, when we are immersed in technology and experiencing it through our own human senses—it can even be "invisible," like Amazon's Alexa. It purchases for us, helps balance our checkbooks, acts as our digital assistant, or maybe just orders dinner. It may also cross the boundary of the physical with implant technologies, like advanced pacemakers, that gather data and support the management of our bodies.

Singularity represents the critical inflection point at which technology becomes embedded in the human experience in a way that renders it not a *physical* thing but an omnipresent part of our lives. Fluidity between technology and human experience will be so absolute that technology itself will appear to fade into the background as it augments, influences, and supports us. Advancements here will continue to build on innovations like sensors, cameras, and Augmented Reality–based technologies.

Singularity creates the opportunity to unlock the power of the human mind and its full potential.

Racing Toward Singularity

We are already starting to see the early stages of Singularity now in a number of innovations in the works to make artificial intelligence more "human," and therefore, more discreet. For example, software company Affectiva is using our facial expressions and the tone of our voices to make AI better at detecting and recognizing emotions such as happiness, anger, and surprise.[3] And companies are making great strides in machine learning—the science of getting computers to act without being directly programmed—making the effect and breadth of technology's influence even more invisible.[4] With this in mind, many countries are investing heavily in AI: China, led by its internet giants Baidu and Alibaba, is investing billions to launch a countrywide effort to make "major breakthroughs" by 2025.[5]

---

3 Erik Brynjolfsson and Andrew McAfee, "The Business of Artificial Intelligence," *Harvard Business Review*, July 2017, https://hbr.org/cover-story/2017/07/the-business-of-artificial-intelligence.

4 Lee Bell, "Machine Learning Versus AI: What's the Difference?" *Wired UK*, December 1, 2016, http://www.wired.co.uk/article/machine-learning-ai-explained.

5 Will Knight, "China's AI Awakening," *MIT Technology Review*, October 10, 2017, https://www.technologyreview.com/s/609038/chinas-ai-awakening/.

Such rapid changes racing forward in technology as we head toward Singularity, particularly in the field of AI, have moved from the realm of science fiction into a hotly debated topic—and some in the tech and science communities have become nervous. They see Singularity as the time when the rise of AI becomes the catalyst for runaway technological growth, potentially leading to the extinction of our species by killer robots and machines. Visionaries such as Elon Musk, Bill Gates, and Stephen Hawking have expressed their fears about AI. Hawking has said we will create machines so intelligent that humankind will have about one hundred years to find another planet.[6] It seems that the plan is to have humanity escape to Mars. And Musk has started two organizations to work for a safer AI and turn it toward good, not evil: the nonprofit OpenAI and Neuralink, which aims to link our brains with computers in an attempt to stop AI from running amok.[7]

Certainly, the regulation of AI is warranted, and like any new technology, there is potential for misuse. That said, it is still a big leap to suggest that AI will become sentient and

---

6 Rex Hupke, "If Stephen Hawking Is Right About Earth's End, Keep an Eye on the Deer," *Chicago Tribune,* May 8, 2017, http://www.chicagotribune.com/news/opinion/huppke/ct-deer-human-bones-huppke-20170508-story.html.
7 Alex Heath, "Elon Musk Has Raised $27 Million to Link Human Brains with Computers," Business Insider, August 25, 2017, http://www.businessinsider.com/elon-musk-neuralink-raises-27-million-2017-8.

destroy humanity. So, there will be a need for regulations and oversight, and no doubt, such restrictions are coming. Echoing our view, some researchers have surmised that, due to the rapid rate of advancements in AI, Singularity could occur as soon as the middle of this century.[8]

But beyond the apocalyptic warnings, a bipartisan group known as the Artificial Intelligence Caucus has been formed by U.S. Representatives John Delaney and Pete Olson to show that the emerging tech could actually be an asset to the public and private sectors, with some governmental foresight. "As lawmakers, our choice is to either get caught flat-footed or to proactively anticipate how things will change and work on smart policies to make sure that the country benefits as much as possible overall," said Delaney on his website.[9,]

Despite so much doom and gloom, we believe Singularity can be a positive opportunity for humanity. And, like previous technological disruptions, Singularity will fuel the ongoing

---

8 Murray Shanahan, *The Technological Singularity* (Cambridge: MIT Press, 2015), https://mitpress.mit.edu/books/technological-singularity.

9 Yu-Ning Aileen Chuang, "Lawmakers: Don't Gauge Artificial Intelligence by What You See in the Movies," National Public Radio podcast, http://www.npr.org/sections/alltechconsidered/2017/10/05/555032943/lawmakers-dont-gauge-artificial-intelligence-by-what-you-see-in-the-movies; "Delaney Launches Bipartisan Artificial Intelligence (AI) Caucus for 115th Congress," press release, May 24, 2017, https://delaney.house.gov/news/press-releases/delaney-launches-bipartisan-artificial-intelligence-ai-caucus-for-115th-congress.

evolution of humanity. In that way, we are more in line with the Artificial Intelligence Caucus than with the alarmists. Singularity will create whole categories of jobs and industries, especially for those who adapt to the new conditions by working to acquire and master needed skills, techniques, and training. Without those, you might have trouble navigating the new customer demand–driven economy.

Experience has taught us that we cannot allow ourselves to get too comfortable, however. General Electric's former CEO Jack Welch said in the 1990s that you have to "eat change for breakfast"—meaning it is necessary to realize that the only constant is change. That is why we are always looking for ways to make ourselves *un*comfortable. Adapting to discomfort is how you make magic happen. The moment you start to feel comfortable is the moment when someone scrappier may be rushing up behind you to gobble up your market share. With technology racing forward, it is likely you will soon face competition you cannot even see right now.

The Future Is Human

We are at a place and time of tremendous economic growth. There is so much progress, and yet people are complaining that they do not have enough work or cannot find employment. How is this possible? People are not taking advantage of opportunities because they have yet to determine how to seize the possibilities. In the interim, automation and robotics are filling the gap. Automation, and potential loss of jobs, are on a lot of people's minds lately. According to a recent survey, nearly two-thirds of U.S. adults believe that most deliveries will soon be made via some form of automated process or robotic drones, and that a majority of stores will be fully automated, involving little human interaction.[10]

That moment appears to be arriving faster than expected. Amazon recently launched its Amazon Go concept, a convenience store with no checkout required: You enter the store with an app, take the items you want off the shelves, and leave. Sensors and other technologies automatically detect and charge you for your purchases.

In another survey, 85 percent of adults said they would support restricting automation to jobs that are dangerous or unhealthy for humans to do. Also, nearly 58 percent agreed there should be definite limits on the number of jobs that companies can supplant with machines.[11]

---

10 "Shareable Facts on Americans' Views and Attitudes Toward Automation Technologies," Pew Research Center, October 4, 2017, http://www.pewinternet. org/2017/10/04/shareable-facts-on-americans-views-and-attitudes-toward-automation-technologies/.

11 John Gramlich, "Most Americans Would Favor Policies to Limit Job and Wage Losses Caused by Automation," Pew Research Center, October 9, 2017, http://www.pewresearch.org/fact-tank/2017/10/09/most-americans-would-favor-policies-to-limit-job-and-wage-losses-caused-by-automation/.

We do not believe automation, robotics, or even AI will be able to duplicate human innovation, vision, and passion. These technologies are far from having any kind of consciousness. Now and into the future, AI will empower humanity to continue training, growing, and investing in learning and ongoing education—because the future is still *human*. In fact, experts say that despite advancements in AI, human beings will be indispensable for jobs that require higher-order critical and innovative thinking and high emotional engagement.[12]

A New Era

As we have expressed, we do not believe that Singularity will signal the end of humanity. We offer a future that is more optimistic and liberating. We believe it will be the beginning of a new era of human creativity. It will empower us to create and innovate like never before. It will be a rebirth for humanity and an opportunity to achieve better things for the world, such as allowing us to create abundant water and energy. And it will free us to achieve greatness by giving us more time to engage in "higher order" activities, such as investing in our relationships and passion projects.

---

12 Ed Hess, "In the AI Age, 'Being Smart' Will Mean Something Completely Different," *Harvard Business Review,* June 19, 2017, https://hbr.org/2017/06/in-the-ai-age-being-smart-will-mean-something-completely-different.

Futurist Ray Kurzweil—also a respected author on Singularity—seems to agree with this assessment. He said, at the recent South by Southwest Conference in Austin, Texas, "We are going to be able to meet the physical needs of all humans. We are going to expand our minds and exemplify these artistic qualities that we value."[13]

The best part of all of this technological change will be just how much it will free us to explore new ways of doing, well, everything. Technology will give us the much-needed time to dig even deeper, be more creative, explore new techniques and processes, and reach new places that we have never even considered.

By way of example, consider a brilliant surgeon. This individual has the expertise, using very precise technique, to perform complex brain surgery, even remove cancerous tumors. With the ability to perform surgeries through robotics and other technological means, this surgeon could devote his time to cancer research and development of new techniques that will be executed via robotics. Such technological advancements are going to rewire societies in terms of how we define value, time, and success; how we consume; how we make money; and how

---

13 Dom Galeon and Christianna Reedy, "Kurzweil Claims That the Singularity Will Happen by 2045," October 5, 2017, futurism.com, https://futurism.com/kurzweil-claims-that-the-singularity-will-happen-by-2045/.

we organize our lives. Technology will enable people to adopt new ways of thinking and interacting across vast distances.

The benefit of embracing this point of view, we believe, is that it is essential to our very survival as a species. There is an opportunity to examine our humanity and our lives, to create better value for the human race, and to solve the grand challenges of reducing poverty and providing universal access to food, water, and power in developing countries. And when we successfully resolve these issues, we will extend life. Global life expectancy will continue to tick upward, as we will be spending more on life sciences research and development. Soon, we will move from sequencing and digitizing *only* tens of millions of human genomes to doing so with billions of human genomes. This major medical breakthrough will push disease prevention and treatment to new levels.

Never before have we focused so intensely on the condition of the planet and climate change; never before have we talked so much about how philosophy plays a part in life and how we must work together to change the human condition. What is left when you have solved hunger, poverty, and lack of power? And what does this mean for the next set of grand challenges we will face? Essentially, we will live in a different world.

There is a crucial benefit to business as well. If you are able to invest in the right technology and catch the right trend at the right time—whether that is solar technology, clean energy, or even space travel—you will help humanity unlock the rewards currently blocked by so many pressing challenges, as we reach Singularity.

CHAPTER THREE

DISRUPTION IS AT THE CORE OF CHANGE

With every age that we have progressed through, from the Pre-Industrial Age to the Digital Age, we have experienced a repeatable, predictable pattern of events that have continued, unvarying, throughout history: Disruptive technologies emerge that affect companies, jobs, and industries, leading to opportunities for reinvention and innovation that ultimately create new realities for humanity. As we have advanced from age to age, our relationship with technology has continually changed as well, from treating technology as a tool for specific tasks, to collaborating with technology in a way that extends us, to—where we are headed as we move toward Digital Singularity—technology becoming a vital and omnipresent part of our lives.

While we may now be in just another "age" with a familiar set of circumstances, we are also in an intense period of continuous change and innovation. We see it when our phones and devices instantly receive updates. Our cars are starting to do this as well: Tesla regularly sends software improvements and bug fixes to its vehicles' operating systems. Change is all around us, but it is the pace of technological innovation over the past two decades that has been most astonishing. And this will only pick up speed in the years ahead.

This constant forward march of technology is part of our collective digital reality. That is why companies need to redouble their efforts to retrain workers, enhance skills, stress continuous education, and learn to adapt to the changing conditions. If you do not have the right tools, and if you are not creating, transforming, or innovating in your industry, you are not competing in the new consumer demand–driven marketplace for business. Only companies that make the right investments—especially in the Technology Prerequisites—will remain relevant and benefit from the robust change around us. Some traditional businesses religiously invest in research and development to improve their performance, products, and services. But when a radical, disruptive technology comes around—like artificial intelligence—it can completely blow away the growth curves.

Disruption Defined

Harvard Business School Professor Clayton Christensen introduced the concept of "disruptive innovation" in 1997 in the pages of the *Harvard Business Review* (and in his book *The Innovator's Dilemma*). He said that *disruption* describes the process by which a smaller company, such as a startup with fewer resources, successfully challenges established industry leaders.[1] In other words, cheaper, simpler, or unanticipated products and services bring down big, incumbent companies. But such companies may not actually be genuinely disruptive in a shifting market. Many define true disruptors as those who create a market where none existed before and appeal to underserved communities before moving on to more mainstream audiences.

While what we generally call a disruption now—like Uber to the taxi industry—may fall slightly outside of Christensen's original definition, we are witnessing again and again examples of companies stuck in older technologies losing their footing, while others offering something entirely new at a different price point surpass them and excel.

If you or your company are still working with outdated *legacy* systems—or worse, employing stubborn "legacy thinking"—

---

1 Clayton M. Christensen, Michael E. Raynor, and Rory McDonald, "What Is Disruptive Innovation?" *Harvard Business Review,* December 2015, https://hbr.org/2015/12/what-is-disruptive-innovation.

you are throwing money away just to keep the lights on. Clinging to older models and outmoded thinking does not allow for innovation, and it could lead to irrelevance soon enough.

Calling a system a "legacy system" implies that its function has not kept up with the times. While legacy systems might serve a great purpose at a specific point of time, more advanced systems and processes are intended to stem from them as our understanding of technology advances. But sometimes, older platforms survive because of the risk and price of replacing them. The cost of moving from outdated platforms can be four to five times the acquisition cost of the original technology. That price tag can present an overwhelming financial hurdle. Acquiring and implementing new technologies can easily range from $200 million to more than $1 billion, with additional expenses for year-over-year maintenance that can be 10–15 percent of the initial cost of the technology.

The problem is, if you do not make investments in technology, with the market moving so quickly—not every year or every four years, but nearly every minute—you may be at risk of drowning under the coming transformational wave. Companies that cannot retool will be disrupted by companies that can. Many companies now cannot even comprehend who their competitors truly are. And there are *invisible* competitors now that they never could have imagined. With that in mind, let us take a look at burgeoning innovations that could soon be disrupting your industry vertical.

The Manufacturing Vertical: 3D Printing

A number of verticals are beginning to be upended by technology advancements. In manufacturing, 3D printing is disrupting, and will continue to disrupt, the supply chain. Take, for example, the common fidget spinner. What was originally sold as a calming toy for children with ADD and ADHD is now made by dozens of manufacturers in China and retails for around $5–$15. There is a supply chain associated with the product, which costs approximately fifty cents to produce. Along the way, the shipper, distributor, and retailer all take their cut. There are people generating value by moving, distributing, and ultimately retailing that fidget spinner.

But what would happen if you could make one yourself at home?

Let us say one of your nephews downloads the design and decides to produce one on a 3D printer at his house. The plastic costs less than a dollar, and he gets the little gears from a local Home Depot for around twenty-five cents. He then sells them to his classmates for $10 each, and they are identical to the ones you would buy online or in a store. What could this simple act do to all the jobs along the way? With a 3D printer, a ten-year-old can now disrupt traditional business.

You can also, technically, 3D-print a house. In fact, the San Francisco-based startup Apis Cor did exactly that in 2017—and in just twenty-four hours for $10,000. Such technology could be a boon to governments that want to quickly and efficiently create whole communities of affordable homes for those who need them most, at a fraction of the regular cost. At present, the process still requires contractors and builders—human workers install, paint, and complete a number of the house's items—but that could change soon enough.[2] The 3D printer alone is an interesting, disruptive technology that could eventually kill off the supply chain for manufacturing products of all sizes and complexity. It has the capacity to render entire categories of manufacturing and consumption obsolete in the U.S., China, and globally.

The Transportation Vertical: Hyperloop

Los Angeles mayor Eric Garcetti reportedly is in active conversations now with busy entrepreneur Elon Musk about using his Boring Company, a new business launched to quickly and inexpensively dig tunnels, to help create new transportation infrastructure. Such tunnels could support another of

---

2 Gene Marks, "This Start-up Will 3D Print Your House…for $10K," *Washington Post,* March 7, 2017, https://www.washingtonpost.com/news/on-small-business/wp/2017/03/07/this-start-up-will-3d-print-your-house-for-10k/?utm_term=.2ba700d9fcff.

Musk's emerging mass transit system projects, the Hyperloop, a pressurized, high-speed mode of transport that could connect cities like Los Angeles to the San Francisco Bay Area. Maryland governor Larry Hogan has also expressed interest and is talking with Musk about constructing a Hyperloop on the East Coast between Washington and New York, with stops in Baltimore and Philadelphia.[3]

The Hyperloop model, which Musk introduced in a 2013 white paper, has been open-sourced to allow different groups to make the concept a reality. Multiple companies are already working on the project. For example, Hyperloop One and Arrivo are vying to build a route between Dubai and Abu Dhabi.[4] The Hyperloop could change the way people, companies, and goods move around the world, although regulations and safety concerns are still being considered.

3 Danielle Muoio, "Maryland's Governor Said to 'Get Ready' for Elon Musk's Hyperloop that Will Connect Baltimore and Washington D.C.," Business Insider, October 19, 2017, http://www.businessinsider.com/elon-musk-hyperloop-maryland-larry-hogan-boring-company-2017-10.
4 Danielle Muoio, "Here's How Hyperloop One's Massive, High-Speed Transport System Will Work," Business Insider, February 20, 2017, http://www.businessinsider.com/hyperloop-one-plan-photos-2017-2/#the-start-up-announced-in-early-novemberthat-it-signed-an-agreement-withdubai-roads-and-transport-authority-to-evaluate-using-the-hyperloop-between-dubai-and-abu-dhabi-1.

If Musk's concept is successful, it could eliminate the need for many to own a car. It could also shift the focus away from traditional public transportation altogether. It could disrupt established transportation systems—trains, trucks, and buses—which could in turn devalue businesses specializing in engines and tires, and possibly even the worldwide trucking and hauling industry. Doing so could have ripple effects on fuel consumption and distribution, and timetables for everything we move vast distances. But it sure would be fun to have coffee with a friend who lives hundreds of miles away from you, without much preplanning. The bigger question is this: If we could transport people and goods in a fraction of the time and cost, why would we not do it?

Financial Services Vertical: Peer-to-Peer Transaction

Like it or not, 2017 was the year of cryptocurrency, a means of exchange that uses encryption to control how much digital currency is created and to verify its transfer.[5] The collaborative technology that makes it all happen is called blockchain. The loss of faith in global central banks, the interest in confidential (and potentially illegal) financial transactions, and a general

---

5 PricewaterhouseCoopers, "Making Sense of Bitcoin, Cryptocurrency and Blockchain," https://www.pwc.com/us/en/financial-services/fintech/bitcoin-blockchain-cryptocurrency.html.

surge of interest with prospectors have been driving interest in cryptocurrencies like Bitcoin and Ethereum, which have increased in value over the last two years.[6] These currencies are largely unregulated and global, and can currently be used to evade taxes and government regulation. This is of concern to governments, since they issue currency—and with cryptocurrency they cannot manage exchange rates or the supply of money.

While regulators move to catch up with these new technologies, cryptocurrencies are gaining in popularity, with major retailers integrating them as an alternative method of payment. Specifically, a number of companies and retailers, such as Microsoft, DISH Network, and Overstock.com, are starting to accept bitcoin as payment for their products.[7]

Such peer-to-peer technology (P2P) platforms allow us to make financial transactions without the interference of regulators. This means that the normal considerations of risk, lending/ underwriting rules, and conflicts of interest may not apply.

---

6 Julie Verhage, "Bitcoin's Epic Rise Leaves Late-1990s Tech Bubble in the Dust," Bloomberg, August 29, 2017, https://www.bloomberg.com/news/ articles/2017-08-29/bitcoin-s-epic-rise-leaves-late-1990s-tech-bubble-in-the-dust.

7 Sean Williams, "5 Brand-Name Businesses That Currently Accept Bitcoin," The Motley Fool, July 6, 2017, https://www.fool.com/investing/2017/07/06/5-brand-name-businesses-that-currently-accept-bitc.aspx.

For individuals, it may be an investment; for others, it may be an opportunity to obtain capital for their business that a bank may not be willing to supply. For example, the Zelle service is a technology that allows people to electronically transfer money from their personal accounts to another registered user via a mobile phone. This system only requires a mobile number and works anywhere within the United States. Zelle is a peer-to-peer (P2P) payment system that resulted from an unpreceded collaboration by more than a half-dozen major banks, including Bank of America and Chase. P2P banking sidesteps many of the government restrictions that apply to traditional banks.

P2P lending technology has also inspired the crowdfunding space: New companies such as PeerStreet and Patch of Land are matching investors with borrowers who flip houses in competitive marketplaces and need financing more quickly than a mortgage broker or bank could ever provide.[8] At present, though, the platforms are only open to investors making at least $250,000 annually, or who have a net worth of $1 million.

Alternative currencies, going back to the barter economy, have long allowed people to exchange without going through banking systems. P2P technology could disrupt financial services

---

8 Marissa Gluck, "Kickstarter-Style Crowdfunding Has Reached House Flipping, and It's Changing How Real Estate Is Sold," *Los Angeles,* October 2017, http://www.lamag.com/mag-features/crowdfunding-real-estate/.

companies by creating a very different competitive landscape, changing clearing, settlement, insurance, and everything in between.[9] If these technologies become pervasive enough, credit card companies eventually could take a hit from lost transaction fees. This would likely change how they operate.

Other Verticals

Disruptions in retail, healthcare, telecommunications, and energy are all possible, as mergers and new technology advancements set the stage for profound change.

- **Retail**: As we have discussed, Amazon Go is on a course to disrupt brick-and-mortar retail by selling goods without any human involvement. While many traditional retailers, such as Macy's, have shut down thousands of stores across the country,[10] grocery store chains may soon start feeling the sting of increased competition as well, as new entrants are beginning to flood the market. One of these, Amazon, purchased Whole Foods, meaning that the company has now closed the loop on the supply chain. It will not only own the physical distribution but it will

---

9 PricewaterhouseCoopers, "Q&A: What's Next for Blockchain's Development?" https://www.pwc.com/us/en/financial-services/publications/qa-whats-next-for-blockchain.html.

10 "Toys 'R' Us Files for Bankruptcy," *The Economist, September 23, 2017,* https://www.economist.com/news/business-and-finance/21729375-rise-e-commerce-did-americas-former-favourite-toys-r-us-files-bankruptcy.

also have physical property and retail outlets, as well as the ability to sell goods and services online.

- **Healthcare**: At present, robotics can refine a surgeon's skillful movements during surgery, similar to how a computer interface helps a plane's pilot smooth out a flight.[11] But in the future, advancements in artificial intelligence could have robots making more autonomous decisions, as well as incisions, independent of humans. By 2025, such surgeries will become the norm, decreasing the number of surgeons required in the operating room. While disruptive to those in the medical profession, it could be highly advantageous for patients due to the availability of new types of microsurgery innovations.

- **Media and entertainment**: Customers of Netflix, Amazon Video, and others have already "cut the cord" in record numbers. In 2017, 22.2 million U.S. adults walked away from cable and satellite TV providers, up 33 percent from the year prior. More than 40 million will snip by 2021,[12] which will be a huge disruption to

11 Emily Williams, "Robotic-Assisted Surgery Reaches for the Future," April 12, 2017, UCLA School of Medicine, http://medschool.ucla.edu/body.cfm?id=1158&action=detail&ref=884.

12 eMarketer, "eMarketer Lowers US TV Ad Spend Estimates as Cord-Cutting Accelerates," September 13, 2017, https://www.emarketer.com/Article/eMarketer-Lowers-US-TV-Ad-Spend-Estimate-Cord-Cutting-Accelerates/1016463.

AT&T, Time Warner, and others. Today, people can get nearly all the content they could ever want without a cable company, saving some $200–$300 per month.

- **Energy**: The advances in solar technology through companies like Solar City, which merged with Tesla in 2016, are shifting the traditional model for selling electricity. And researchers at MIT are now experimenting with a new device that turns sunlight into heat and converts it back into light. The process—expected to be viable within ten to fifteen years—could be twice as efficient as regular solar panels in providing cheap, continuous power.[13] The key question becomes whether the utilities of today will continue to exist two decades from now, as it will not be economically viable for them to maintain power lines and last-mile connections.

As we are seeing, many industries will be shaped by developing and evolving combinations of technologies. We are moving into a paradigm of rapid, continuous innovation—a period unlike any we have experienced in human history—that will stir reinvention in some fields and present remarkable opportunities for many more as we near Singularity.

---

13 James Temple, "10 Breakthrough Technologies: Hot Solar Cells," *MIT Technology Review*, March/April 2017, https://www.technologyreview.com/ s/603497/10-breakthrough-technologies-2017-hot-solar-cells/.

One thing is certain: We are living in an on-demand society. Need to know something? Go on Google. With information, goods, and services at our fingertips, a desire to return to simplicity is emerging amid all this technological change. When all of our needs are instantaneously met, we will return to where human beings were a century ago, when we spent more time reflecting, reading, and communicating with one another. People will explore, debate, and argue again. They will do all the things we once did at the dinner table decades ago—activities that we have not done nearly enough in the last thirty years. The new digital technology investment requirements for business will eventually give us an opportunity to be reborn. In the chapters to come, we will explore the technology pillars that will enable this shift and transform businesses.

CHAPTER FOUR

HYPERCONVERGENCE: EXPONENTIAL CHANGE BY COMBINING TECHNOLOGIES

As we approach Singularity, innovation is sprinting forward and how we relate to and interact with technology is evolving. But generations ago, things were different. In the Industrial Age, tools and technology had a specific purpose, like a shoeing hammer that helped make horses roadworthy. We picked up the tool, used it just for its task, and laid it down when we were done. We did not have a *relationship* with it, and we did not think much about it. It had one function: to make the task at hand more efficient.

A lot has changed since then, as we have moved from age to age. We are now more closely connected to our *digital* tools. We depend on them, and they enable us to live deeper, fuller, more capable lives. Our devices interact with us, "check up on us" by keeping tabs on our health, and allow us to express our creativity and exchange ideas with others across the world. In the near future, these digital tools will not only help us live better, they will act in a *predictive* manner: alerting a doctor when we are sick, automatically making sure we never run out of basic necessities, and jumping into action to contact plumbers and painters when a leaking bathtub spills onto the floors below. Digital Singularity—the omnipresence of technology—will change the way we live and work.

In Chapter 2, we learned about the Technology Prerequisites, innovations that businesses need to start investing in now. When combined, these technologies create the breakthroughs that will help define the new economy. We have called these new innovations the technology pillars of the age. In the Information Age, from the prerequisites that included the World Wide Web, global networks, and PCs and tablets, the pillars became data storage, business and personal applications, and high-bandwidth networks. In this new Digital Age, these four pillars will allow us to define Digital Singularity. Some of these technological solutions exist today in a nascent stage; others are on the verge of breakthroughs. They form the second ring of our graphic, the *"Four Pillars of Digital Singularity."* The

Humanity's Relationship with Technology through the Ages

Human Ages	Technology Prerequisites	Pillars of the Age	Rules of the Economy
Digital Singularity (Digital Age)	Cloud IoT Sensors Artificial Intelligence RPA Blockchain Cyber Security 3D Printing	Hyper-Convergence Digital Moments Augmented Reality Digital Twins	Barrier-free Access Democratized Egalitarianism The Sharing Economy Transboundary Communities
Information Age	Mobile Phones PCs and Tablets Email Global Networks World Wide Web	Data Storage Business & Personal Applications High Bandwidth Networks	Electronic transactions Equal access to information Social Media Real time communications
Industrial Age	Radio, telegraph and television Centralized Electric Power and Utilities Fossil Fuel and Steam Engines Rail, Car, Ship and Airplane transportation	Global Broadcasting Mass Production and Machine Automation Transportation Advances	Access to electric power Access to running water Birth of modern medicine Global Economy is born
Pre-Industrial Age	Fire Wheel Early Tools	Agriculture Hunting	Trading persists over currency Subsistence level of living

Singularity

Symbiosis

Master/Slave

Core Elements of the Digital Economy

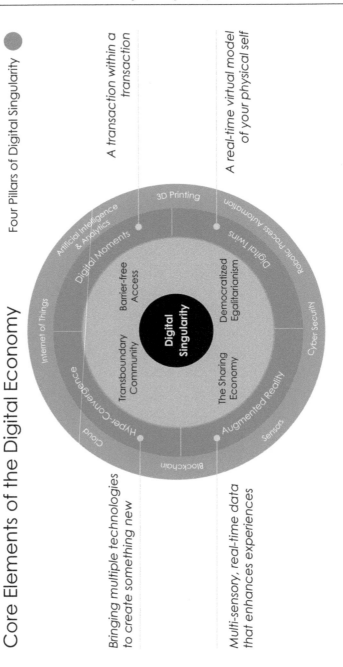

Four Pillars of Digital Singularity

A transaction within a transaction

A real-time virtual model of your physical self

Bringing multiple technologies to create something new

Multi-sensory, real-time data that enhances experiences

first, *Hyperconvergence*, is the foundation upon which we will build our discussion of the remaining three technological trends over the course of the next three chapters: Digital Moments, Augmented Reality, and Digital Twins.

Understanding Hyperconvergence

To truly grasp the meaning of Hyperconvergence, we must first understand each of the Technology Prerequisites for a digital ecosystem. Technologies such as Wi-Fi, the cloud, sensors, and 3D printing, when combined, act to augment the original technology. To this end, we define Hyperconvergence as the seamless merging of two or more independent technologies, which may have different, distinct uses, to create something entirely new and unique with an enhanced function that is greater than the original technologies could ever have by themselves.

With Hyperconvergence, the original device has a new purpose. The "smart" refrigerator is no longer just a rectangular machine to keep food cold; it is now a device to manage our intake of healthy foods and help us achieve our diet goals. It has a greater purpose. A running shoe is no longer defined simply by its ability to protect our feet as we jog down the street. With a sensor in its sole and Wi-Fi, it becomes a device to monitor our exercise and well-being—how far and how fast we run, how hard our arches and toes are hitting the pavement, and our endurance. It ceases to be seen and used as just a shoe.

The new forms of these items fundamentally change how we have used and viewed them for generations and now have a greater purpose than their legacy counterparts alone. This is the promise of Hyperconvergence.

At the most basic level, consider the "smart" watch, which is becoming more popular by the day. If it just told time, that would not be anything different than what watches have been doing for hundreds of years, ever since the 1700s when large pocket or necklace watches came into use because people wanted to carry the time around with them. A smart watch maintains its original function, but with its connection to the internet, for the first time in hundreds of years, its purpose has shifted. It has been redefined. Now, it has the ability to sync with our calendar, remind us of our meetings, manage communications, and even track our fitness and health, like collecting data on our heart rate and all of our movement in a day, whether we are running, moving, or standing. The simple convergence of two common technologies gives birth to a completely new device with new capabilities and functions that are far beyond what early clock builders could ever have originally intended. This may seem unremarkable today, as much of this technology is commonplace, but comprehending the phenomenon of combining the Technology Prerequisites with existing technology can help explain the rapid and exponential opportunity with Hyperconvergence.

As we are seeing, a "multiplier" effect happens with Hyper-convergence that extends beyond the technologies themselves. An exponential growth in value exceeds the sum of the parts. This multiplier effect is the essence of Hyperconvergence—hence the prefix *hyper*, from the Greek *huper*, meaning "over" or "beyond." Convergence, alone, is the merging of technologies; Hyperconvergence implies that we are accelerating the ability to generate opportunities.

The Smart Thermostat

Today, many devices are connected to the cloud, allowing them to function within the emerging "Internet of Things" (IoT). The industry for connected objects is exploding. It has been projected that by 2020, there will be nearly 200 billion connected "things," many of them in businesses, factories, and healthcare.[1] On a basic level, this new technology combines sensor-rich devices, off-the-shelf products, and the internet. The result of this combination of multiple technologies is Hyperconvergence. Some of the simplest examples can be seen in what companies are doing today with Wi-Fi, cameras, and other technologies. Traditional items, from clothing to appliances to phones, have

---

1 Intel, "A Guide to the Internet of Things," https://www.intel.com/content/www/us/en/internet-of-things/infographics/guide-to-iot.html; IDC, "Connecting the IoT: The Road to Success," infographic, https://www.idc.com/infographics/IoT.

suddenly become something exceptional—something *smart* that can, to some extent, operate in an interactive and autonomous manner. Hyperconvergence is a blank slate on which to conceive a unique technology to be used in a unique way. Many surprising and extraordinary innovations are possible when we take off-the-shelf equipment and apply ingenuity.

Wi-Fi enabled thermostats provide an interesting example of the difference Hyperconvergence can make. These devices enable us to do more than just check and control the temperature in our homes with a phone app—there is that multiplier effect at work that affects the entire grid, and the consumers and companies that are part of it.

If you decide to "opt in" with your device, it now can be connected to the national grid, enabling it to share data it collects about your power usage with your local utility. The power company may end up utilizing this data to develop analytics of usage patterns to predict surges and prevent power outages. Your thermostat could be programmed to support your off-peak and on-peak use in a manner that reduces your electricity consumption, and could even double capacity without adding a single watt of energy use, all by rerouting power.[2]

2 Vivek Ranadive, "Hyperconnectivity: The Future Is Now," *Forbes,* February 19, 2013, https://www.forbes.com/sites/vivekranadive/2013/02/19/ hyperconnectivity-the-future-is-now/#642c0b8530ad.

So, if a surge happens on a hot summer day, the utility could give you a discount not to turn on your air conditioner during that time. Or perhaps, the utility could switch off your unit to conserve electricity on the grid.

The device could also connect with other devices to provide long-term analytics on the smart grid and point to areas where additional infrastructure needs to be built. In essence, disparate technologies—a $5 Wi-Fi extender, the cloud, and a $60 thermostat—now combine to fashion a smart-enabled way to analyze and manage regional power consumption. This kind of convergence could save millions of dollars when applied to a broad range of users. This device is no longer a thermostat; it is an energy-monitoring tool designed to support the optimization of regional energy consumption. This is what happens with Hyperconvergence.

Other Uses

There are possibilities for Hyperconvergence everywhere. Consider your mobile phone. You are probably walking around with a smartphone in your pocket—a device more powerful than all the technology NASA used to send the Apollo 11 astronauts to the moon in 1969. Today's mobile phones are full of sensors, accelerometers, gyroscopes, barometers, and other tech that can be enabled to hyperconverge any activity or repeatable process and provide data to others that can be multiplied. They have the ability to send information remotely—and that means they are coordinating geolocation, the real-world geographic coordinates and location of an object. As we have seen, this technology is already being used to help manage traffic congestion, to remember where you have parked your car at the mall, and even to help businesses decide where to launch their stores or offices. All of our traditional and emerging technologies present limitless opportunities for Hyperconvergence when merged with the right set of technologies—and the growth of these opportunities is picking up speed every day, driven by the power of data.

Other examples of hyperconverged innovations are just as fascinating, and vary in complexity:

- Getting your children to brush their teeth regularly can be quite challenging. But it might become easier with the Magik smart toothbrush. It is a brushing experience driven by a motivational Augmented Reality game that uses a phone's front-facing camera and the brush's motion-tracking and sensor technologies so kids can "shoot" bubbles at cavity-causing monsters on the app. The aim of the brush is to put kids on the right path toward good oral hygiene and overall health. The toothbrush collects and sends data to parents about when and how long their children brush. Could this device eventually have kids playing against others in the same age group in some kind of "brushing Olympics?" And could the collected data be sent to their dentist to enhance dental care techniques and help prevent gingivitis across a spectrum of children worldwide?

- Handlebars on bicycles have served a fairly basic purpose since they first burst onto the scene in nineteenth-century Europe: to provide steering control for the two wheels. This hardware is getting a new function and purpose with Velco's Wink Bar smart handlebar: GPS provides geolocation in case of theft; it also provides turn-by-turn guidance, and integrated sensors turn on the bike's light when it gets dark. It is all controlled via an app. Could law enforcement or public advocacy groups one day use data gathered by the smart device to curtail bike thefts? Could city governments use the GPS geolocation technology data of all bicycles in an urban area to create real-time maps to cut down on accidents, especially between cars and bikes?

- NASA has been experimenting with 3D printing for everything from parts and tools to fabrics and food on the ground and in space. Of course, 3D printing itself is an amalgam of products that yields a new technology: a scanner, modeling software, and a computer and monitor.

NASA's engineers recently printed, with metals and other materials, a large part for a rocket engine, with an eye toward decreasing costs for future engines. NASA has already been testing a zero-gravity 3D printer at the International Space Station to print tools, such as ratchet wrenches. It could soon 3D-print new, space-age fabrics used for antennas and to protect spacecraft from things like meteorites. It is also working on printing pizzas for astronauts to make in space. These methods could potentially trim the time and resources needed to manufacture in space by sending rockets back and forth.[3] The European Space Agency is working on 3D printing as well to erect buildings and residential dwellings on the moon and Mars. This hyperconverged technology could eventually affect industrialization and help enable colonization of other planets. If all of these 3D printing methods are successful and utilized, the space agencies could potentially cut out the manufacturing and supply chain channels of many companies for parts, fabrics, and materials.

In these examples we have seen the transformative nature of what is materializing here: a vast world of infinite

---

3 Elizabeth Howell, "SpaceX Taking 3D Printing to the Final Frontier," Space. com, August 21, 2014, https://www.space.com/26899-spacex-3d-printing-rocket-engines.html.

possibilities—and a world of infinite *efficiency* creation. In the near future, hyperconverged products will likely work like this:

- Your car checks in with your mobile phone and email, recognizes you are going on a long road trip, creates an alert, and charges itself—or goes to the gas station for an auto-refill. The gas station is automatically chosen based on the nearest location where the best-rated and lowest-priced fuel is being sold.

- Your refrigerator sees you are low on milk, eggs, and oranges and automatically orders them from the online grocer, which delivers them the next day.

If you are still wondering how all this applies to you and your business, think of it this way: Companies that do not focus on how to adopt the technology pillars in their business plans, as their competitors surely will, could soon find themselves falling behind the curve in this Digital Age as we head toward Singularity. Many of the world's top companies are being challenged by tech innovator giants, and by 2027, at the current churn rate, 75 percent of the S&P 500 will be replaced.[4] Nearly half of MIT's Top 50 Disruptive Companies

---

4 Scott D. Anthony, S. Patrick Viguerie, Evan I. Schwartz, and John Van Landeghem, "2018 Corporate Longevity Forecast: Creative Destruction Is Accelerating," Innosight, https://www.innosight.com/insight/creative-destruction-whips-through-corporate-america-an-innosight-executive-briefing-on-corporate-strategy/.

have launched within the past ten years.[5] To remain competitive, companies should think like disruptors, investing in innovations and reinvention measures that drive them forward to defend against any potential upstarts.[6]

We are beginning to see that anything that has hyperconverged is more efficient, many factors faster, and able to provide solutions, utilities, and services that were heretofore unimaginable. The resulting technology is immensely more productive and interactive with customers[7] and helps to accelerate decision-making by weeding out inefficiencies[8] while driving global alignment.[9] Such new efficiencies could also increase the reach of supply chains, better connecting customers, manufacturers, and retailers.[10] The information

---

5 Nina Curley, "Why Companies Should Embrace Disruption," World Economic Forum, January 6, 2015, https://www.weforum.org/agenda/2015/01/why-companies-should-embrace-disruption/.

6 Curley, "Why Companies Should Embrace Disruption."

7 Tom Brewster, "When Machines Take Over: Our Hyperconnected World," BBC, January 25, 2014, http://www.bbc.com/capital/story/20140124-only-connect.

8 Oracle, "The New Hyperconnected Enterprise," http://www.oracle.com/us/industries/communications/hyperconnected-enterprise-brief-2421041.pdf.

9 John Fredette, Revital Marom, Kurt Steinert, and Louis Witters, "The Promise and Peril of Hyperconnectivity for Organizations and Societies," World Economic Forum, http://www3.weforum.org/docs/GITR/2012/GITR_Chapter1.10_2012.pdf.

10 Fredette et al., "The Promise and Peril of Hyperconnectivity."

we can obtain by hyperconverging traditional technologies presents countless opportunities, and if they are not doing so already, your competitors will soon be using this information to drive sales, revenue, and new client business.

Hyperconvergence at the B2B Level

Technology is disrupting many business verticals, and will continue to do so. As we have seen, traditional brick-and-mortar retail businesses have been sliding toward irrelevance for some time now—especially those not adopting new technologies. One thing is clear: adopting a data- and technology-driven model is one way to avoid obsolescence.

At a macro level, Amazon's recent purchase of Whole Foods is a prime example of how Hyperconvergence can also occur at the business-to-business level (B2B). In this example, a technology company merged with an organization that followed a traditional business model, thus creating added value. This affects the entire industry, and we can see the multiplier effect in action. By combining brick-and-mortar retail stores with a virtual marketplace for products and a vast distribution system, the online giant sent shockwaves through the grocery industry. On its first day of ownership, Amazon lowered some prices by as much as 43 percent—addressing a sticking point for many consumers, who called Whole Foods

"Whole Paycheck."[11] Stocks for Amazon's competitors are beginning to inch down, as investors believe they will not be able to beat Amazon/Whole Foods on cost and reach. Amazon has also integrated its supply chain systems with Whole Foods, which now operates on a more modern platform.

Beyond pricing, Amazon is expected to leverage its impressive digital expertise to collect and connect the data it gets from stores and social media. This could allow it to analyze consumption patterns for all kinds of foods and find ways to further improve the efficiency of its entire supply chain. The act of combining storefronts with on-the-cloud data from registers could change how we think about food—what we eat, how it is stocked, where it is made available, and how we get the products that end up in our homes. The grocery industry and other related verticals will be affected by the growth of this technology for many years to come.

Amazon, a company that has never had retail outlets or made its own products, is disrupting retail, and its actions could influence how the entire industry does business now and into Singularity.

---

11 Jennifer Kaplan and Matthew Boyle, "Amazon Cuts Whole Foods Prices as much as 43% on First Day," Bloomberg, August 8, 2017, https://www.bloomberg.com/news/articles/2017-08-28/amazon-cuts-prices-at-whole-foods-as-much-as-50-on-first-day.

It is not only large supermarkets that are starting to feel the effects of Hyperconvergence. Smaller chains and companies actually stand to gain the most because they will be able to compete on an even playing field. For example, Thrive Market, a membership-based company that delivers healthy foods and products at wholesale prices, is gaining market share, especially among the coveted target group of millennials. Thrive Market may just be a small startup now, with $111 million raised in 2016,[12] but it is using data like its bigger competitors. It has optimized its supply chain model to offer customers discounts on items they like, and will ship directly to their homes. It also tracks customers' purchase history, makes recommendations based on what they have bought in the past—and even projects when they are low on things like kale or almond milk.

You do not have to be a supermarket behemoth with thousands of locations and billions in sales to be able to use transaction data from your customers. The moment you hyperconverge your cash registers with other forms of technology is your first opportunity to learn what your customers really want. If you are not collecting data, you may end up losing market share.

---

12 Ariana Marini, "Thrive Market's Founder Turned His Passion into a Successful Business. Here's What You Can Learn from Him," A Plus, August 21, 2017, http://aplus.com/a/thrive-market-gunnar-lovelace-business-advice?no_monetization=true.

Hyperconvergence makes technology disruption a possibility for everyone. But if you do not start adapting to new forms of technology, your business may not even be around to see the dawn of Singularity. And that means you will not have a chance to participate in the new, emerging digital economy.

CHAPTER FIVE

DIGITAL MOMENTS: TRANSACTIONS WITHIN TRANSACTIONS

So, you live in Los Angeles and you are going to meet an old friend for coffee. You grew up together, and as with many older, established relationships, you feel a sense of obligation to keep ties. But whenever you meet this person, you come out feeling drained. People can have an impact on our emotional state. Some interactions can be highly motivating, while others can be very taxing. Unfortunately, most of us do not maintain analytics on our feelings as we go through the day. But if we could understand how the external world affects our emotional state, we might be able to better design our interactions to drive a higher level of satisfaction and happiness.

Enter Bliss, a new, innovative app due to hit the market. Bliss syncs with your smartphone's calendar and uses elements of artificial intelligence and data analytics to help you achieve a more positive outlook. Much like a fitness app can help you stay on your exercise plan, Bliss tracks your emotional state during key interactions throughout your day. So, after the coffee meeting with your friend, the app might send you a message asking, "How was your meeting with your friend? Can you rate your experience?" You are given three colors to describe your state of mind: green, yellow, or red. You choose red. The app then asks you, "Why was it bad?" You answer: "He was really negative, telling me what I should do with my life." Over time, the app would be able to provide you with recommendations on meetings and their frequency. So, the next time you want to meet this friend, the app might remind you, "The last three times you met Dave, you felt very angry or drained." The app may continue, "Should I postpone your meeting or shorten it to thirty minutes?" The app then provides feedback on your emotional state to encourage activities that are positive and drive your desired state of mind. As time goes on, the app becomes smarter and continues to monitor your calendar events and follow up with you. Soon, it recognizes additional trends and makes recommendations, such as, "Consider going to the yoga class this evening. It always makes you feel great." This technology is designed to help you make better decisions and to live in a more healthy, balanced manner.

In essence, Bliss uses information about us and analytics in a very sophisticated way to help us conduct healthier "transactions." These transactions occur as we are living our day-to-day lives. They happen automatically as Bliss continues to analyze our calendar, meetings, and activities. It also uses positive psychology to help us become the best possible versions of ourselves.[1]

The process that the app offers is an interesting example of the second pillar of Singularity, *Digital Moments*: a transaction that occurs within a transaction. Digital Moments can happen anywhere, in the background, and simultaneously with other activities. That means that while we are doing an activity—like rating a visit with an old friend—another action is transpiring without human prompting. This is enabled through automation, analytics, and artificial intelligence. These transactions are collecting data and information and are doing *something* with it, like providing you with useful feedback, such as, "Should I take future visits with the old friend off your calendar?" And you may not necessarily even be aware *when* it is happening, or *how* it is happening,

---

1 Bliss corporate page, http://bliss31.com/about.php.

but this subtransaction is moving forward automatically. A digital moment is also a form of robotic process automation. Once you add RPA and predictive analytics, it becomes a different experience.

A digital moment has five characteristics:

1. It is a *transaction*. It is a digital activity that is happening concurrently while you are doing something else. This could be a purchase, a communication, or any transaction between two parties.

2. It is *automatic*. Transactions automatically happen with the given information, without any prompting.

3. It requires *consent*. These transactions happen with the individual's consent, which may have been given at a prior time or in real time during the transaction.

4. It is *secure*. The transaction is secure and utilizes encryption or biometrics prior to approval.

5. It utilizes *social media*. The transaction may permit the collection of feedback, ratings, and preferences.

These Digital Moments will become more and more a part of our lives as we head toward Singularity.

Types of Transactions

As we saw in the Bliss example, Digital Moments can change your behavior and affect your lifestyle. But the initial transaction does not only provide you with information—it actually triggers another type of transaction. The first could be something as simple as an activity, like riding your bike. The next action could be you moving from Point A to Point B, but during that time, your Wi-Fi-connected bike is sending out useful data about your riding patterns, which could prove useful for analyzing your overall health or adjusting your workout. The act of riding sparks another automated transaction.

In Chapter 3, we discussed the smart thermostat as an example of a Hyperconvergence of technologies to create something new. But it is also a digital moment. When you turn up the thermostat on a cold day, the device relays data back to the utility, which could send an email or text notification that says, "These are peak hours. Are you sure you want to boost the temperature?" By adjusting your thermostat, the utility instantly launches an effort to alter your behavior, encouraging you to purchase energy during off-peak hours, to heat your home when it is cheaper to do so—which helps it manage power consumption across a vast area.

Digital Moments can also be e-commerce-related, factored into the process of buying a product. All of your transactions and purchases are analyzed, and your preferences are noted. That means the next time you need to make a purchase, an e-tailer will automatically know that you need something and will show you the best options available in the market. Your previous purchases will automatically trigger new options for you.

Let us look at another toothbrush example. An electric toothbrush is a tool many of us use each day. We know these devices have heads that need to be replaced every few months. If you had a smart, connected toothbrush, you would not have to pay attention to the bristles fading from blue to white. After checking your usage patterns, the toothbrush could automatically send a notification to your Amazon account to order a new brush head—without your prompting. The replacement head would arrive at your doorstep by drone sometime later that day.

Digital Moments could change the way we watch television in the years ahead. Let us say a big English soccer match is happening: Leeds is playing Sheffield. You are watching the game and notice that one of the players is wearing a style of shoe you really like (you play soccer in a local league). You could pause the game, select "like" on the shoes on the TV, and quickly scan through the starred ratings and reviews of them. The TV would then search for them online at the best price. Soon, there is an indication from the online store that you can buy these shoes directly from your TV. It could also happen automatically, as long as you have authorized this type of transaction in advance. And since your whole home would be "smart," the TV also notices there is a small defect in how it is processing colors and schedules a system upgrade for a time when the set is idle. It even puts together a list of local repair companies specializing in this issue, just in case the upgrade does not fix the problem—and would ask you to choose one the next time you turn on the TV.

With regard to brands and prices, since we will instantly be given the best price on a product, will we care who makes it? In the near future, the quality of commodities will be so high, we likely will not. At one time, there was a major difference among, for example, different brands of toothbrushes. Today, however, whatever qualitative differences remain between toothbrushes are negligible. Will the consumers of the future really care who makes them? Probably not. Saving money will be their top concern. So, brand loyalty will suffer—in fact, it may not even exist.

All of these movements are wrapped up in Digital Moments, transactions within transactions. They make up a layer of activity that is nearly invisible to you, happening five times a second, hundreds of thousands of times a day. Digital Moments will simplify many transactions and enable you to more easily get the products and services you want.

A New Way of Doing Business

Like Hyperconvergence, Digital Moments are a foundational concept that we will need to understand to talk more broadly about the subjects in upcoming chapters, such as Transboundary Communities and Barrier-free Access, two Rules of the New Economy. Digital Moments also help us answer the question, "Why does Hyperconvergence matter?" It is significant because when you can bring together two unique technologies to make a new product, anyone can be a competitor. And in the global marketplace, everybody can battle for market share and audience.

So, how can companies and individuals take advantage of these Digital Moments? You have to be aware that the go-to-market channels for selling your product have shifted. That means you need to sell your product differently and understand what a digital moment is so that you can tailor your approach to this new mode of selling. There will still be brick-and-mortar stores in the years ahead—people will walk into grocery stores and buy food as they do now. But there will be other ways, through Digital Moments, to automate demand generation and increase customer awareness.

For example, consider what is happening now in social media. When you spend time scrolling through your Facebook newsfeed, you might see a number of ads for products that you recently viewed across different sites, including a purse that looks very similar to one that you purchased on nordstrom. com. In this case, the digital moment is occurring on different levels. The first transaction is the act of scanning your newsfeed, likes, and other searched content that you have clicked on in the past across various sites. When you see a product on your newsfeed, it has been curated and strategically placed in front of you to prompt you to buy it. This type of demand generation, made possible by Technology Prerequisites, is a new sales avenue. Increasingly, partnerships between strong technology and analytics-driven companies, such as Facebook, and more traditional companies, such as Nordstrom, will be necessary to retain market share. In this case, Nordstrom would pay to be a featured brand on Facebook.

A digital moment, like Hyperconvergence, creates the possibility of additional transactions that together can drive a richer experience and greater value. Ultimately, as a user, we receive more value out of this digital experience. Facebook, for example, permits multiple actions to be completed at the same time, like browsing your newsfeed for posts from your friends and purchasing a new purse.

Building Loyalty in a Different Way

We are defining terms like Hyperconvergence and Digital Moments because we want you to think about how to incorporate them into your day-to-day life. You will soon realize that when you want to sell "the next great thing," you should strategically think, "How do we take advantage of Digital

Moments as market channels to sell our products?" Some of the value is in analytics; some of it is in the data being collected that produces automatic transactions that change people's lives.

Since Digital Moments are microtransactions that are happening continuously, they are improving our analytics. If you are selling a product, you have the opportunity to better understand what people like and do not like, since they are regularly interacting with you (assuming you have technologies that are analyzing this data). That could help you tweak your marketing and sales channels, because you will understand customer preferences. Microtransactions and microadvertising allow companies to leverage their marketing dollars in the most focused, targeted way to get the right message to the right audience.

Digital Moments will become a revenue-generating model for companies and the norm for how we relate to products and services as we head toward Singularity. They will create a long tail of commerce to build and retain customers. And, in some instances, if you opt in, the company will not even need your permission every time it wants to resell to you. When the product or feedback arrives, you will be happy you were not asked to be a part of the series of events that led to its delivery. This will create opportunities for consumption-oriented inter-actions *in the moment*, without the user having to make a list, drive to the store, make a purchasing decision, pick up the products, or bring them home. In the future, more consumers will be using their mobile phones, smart televisions, and other devices to access opportunities for consumption or interaction.

Digital Moments are microtransactions, microcommunications, micro-*anything* that happens within another transaction. And yes, they can be another go-to-market channel to communicate with people, and another way to promote your products and services. Digital Moments are a way to evangelize anything—they are a communication medium and a way to "sell" the merits of your company.

If you do not start learning about Digital Moments, you could lose sales to this new channel. You likely already have begun to do so, and that loss is only going to accelerate. If retail corporations are not selling this way, sooner or later they will be missing out on a large segment of the market. The good news is that you can jump into this channel and be a part of it—but only if you acknowledge its existence.

CHAPTER SIX

AR: COMBINING PHYSICAL AND DIGITAL WORLDS TO CREATE ENHANCED EXPERIENCES

n 1984's *Terminator*, Arnold Schwarzenegger's cyborg from the future scans a red-tinted room that is superimposed with data and objects to help it identify what it is "seeing": people, animals, distance between objects, the heartbeat of individuals in range, and threat levels. Today, tech enthusiasts are giving instructions online for how to recreate this view using headsets like Microsoft's HoloLens—wearable, mixed-reality goggles that allow users to interact with digital content and holograms that appear in their natural field of vision.

The tech may not be as sophisticated as what the Terminator saw, but we are on our way to using *Augmented Reality*

(AR) to do more than just scan and identify objects in a sci-fi movie. Eventually this technology will help supply chains, warehouses, medical experts, and any number of other applications.

So, what is Augmented Reality? It is similar to virtual reality (VR) in that both alter our view of the world, but there are key functional differences between the two. Virtual reality is an immersive experience that involves putting on a physical device, which takes you to a world that may or may not exist. It could be a video game or a flight simulator, but the user interacts in a purely virtual world. Qantas Airways offers an inflight VR experience that allows the user to explore the Great Barrier Reef's Hamilton Island in an immersive 360-degree video before the plane even touches down.

In AR, we are still interacting with the actual world around us, but we are getting data, inputs, computer-generated images, and sound that supplement our perception of our surroundings and enhance analog experiences. It allows predictive decision-making in real time through analytics that enable people to obtain information rapidly and efficiently. So, instead of merely exploring realms in your VR glasses, you could look out the airplane window and receive information about what you are seeing, rather than just viewing rows of nonspecific, tiny buildings tens of thousands of feet below you. Your AR view could also help you understand that there is cloud cover and let you know if it is raining below, as well as the temperature outside, the local time, if you are nearing a city, and how long your flight will actually take.

Another example would be a factory worker wearing AR glasses who picks up a part used to build a car. The glasses scan the part and identify it either as functional or defective, depending on whether it meets the correct dimensions and specifications. The naked eye, alone, could not have provided this type of data and would likely have missed any slight imperfections. The technology makes the worker's job easier and the finished product is of better quality.

Augmented Reality takes the information we would normally get from our senses—from the real world, in real time—and enhances it with external technology so we can make decisions based on the inputs. The analytics and additional information it provides allow us to make better decisions immediately. One thing to keep in mind is that AR is not possible without sensor technology. The sensors detect the malfunctioning part that the auto worker is holding in that specific work environment. Then, the sensors send signals to the auto worker and pertinent information is displayed on the AR glasses for next steps. Sensors heighten our perception and gather real-world interactions to formulate a digital model to execute desired output.

We have seen AR technology in action many times: The NFL was an early adopter of Augmented Reality in the late 1990s, projecting a yellow first-down line on the field under the players' movements that only viewers at home could see. Since then, a number of smartphone geolocation apps have become available that allow us to see superimposed characters on the regular landscape.[1] Snapchat Lens has been employing simple examples of AR, enabling us to overlay filters and emojis on landscapes and even our bodies—putting a dog's nose and ears on your face, for example.[2] It also launched a 3D art platform, where users could see works of art, from artists like Jeff Koons, by holding up their phones in certain locations.[3] Pokemon Go, which stirred up interest in AR in 2016, put the technology to use in a similar way, mixing the physical and digital worlds as a social experience.[4]

---

1 Tim Perdue, "Applications of Augmented Reality," Lifewire, July 7, 2017, https://www.lifewire.com/applications-of-augmented-reality-2495561.

2 Swapna Krishna, "Snapchat Adds 3D Bitmoji to Its Augmented Reality Features," Engadget, September 14, 2017, https://www.engadget.com/2017/09/14/snapchat-3d-bitmoji-world-lens-ar/.

3 Josh Constine, "Snap to Launch Augmented Reality Art Platform Tomorrow," Techcrunch, October 2, 2017, https://techcrunch.com/2017/10/02/snapchat-art/.

4 Om Malik, "Pokemon Go Will Make You Crave Augmented Reality," *The New Yorker,* July 12, 2016, https://www.newyorker.com/tech/elements/pokemon-go-will-make-you-crave-augmented-reality.

Beyond apps and games, we are already using AR in our cars every day: Our vehicles are gaining more and more AR enhancements and will continue to build in complexity as we head toward Singularity. The simplest application is when we shift into reverse and the screen on the vehicle's dashboard "paints" moving lines over our view of what is behind us to guide us in getting in and out of parking spaces. Some cars now come equipped with "head-up displays" on the front windshield, using a range of cameras, project information—speed, navigation directions, road lanes in any lighting condition, and other objects just out of our field of vision—that make our drive to the supermarket safer. Soon, cars will include advanced head-up displays that will plant a "ghost car" in front of us that we will follow for navigation, as well as a system to warn about pedestrians crossing the street in busy, urban environments. The technology will also sense the deceleration of cars on the road in front of us to help us maneuver and avoid impending accidents. Blind spots may become a thing of the past through the use of multiple cameras that project onto "transparent" columns in our cars.[5]

The recent resurgence of Google Glass, the device that popularized the concept of "smart" eyewear, presents a good

---

5 Casey Williams, "Head Up Display Systems Project a Vision of the Future," *Chicago Tribune*, August 24, 2015, http://www.chicagotribune.com/classified/automotive/sc-cons-0827-autotips-head-up-displays-20150821-story.html.

example of how companies and workers could be using AR technology in the years ahead. Google Glass, a head-mounted display designed in the shape of eyeglasses, debuted to consumers in 2014. It allowed us to view many functions on computers overlaid on the lens. More than fifty businesses, including Boeing and Volkswagen, use the newer 2.0 enterprises version on the factory floor as a hands-free device that supplies real-time instructions, checklists, and diagrams to aid workers assembling complex parts and wiring. Operated with voice commands, it increases efficiency and safety by cutting down time spent entering data or reading instructions.[6] The market will keep growing for such glasses, too: by 2025, about 14.4 million U.S. workers are expected to wear smart glasses.[7]

Like the other pillars so far, AR will likely be monetized in some way. Wearing AR glasses or goggles will allow us to interact with the world in a different way. That means Digital Moments can connect you to different transactions—you will be able to buy things that you see, instead of searching for them. See a pair of shoes someone is wearing that you like? You will be able to purchase them through a type of digital

6 Steven Levy, "Google Glass 2.0 Is a Startling Second Act," *Wired,* July 18, 2017, https://www.wired.com/story/google-glass-2-is-here/.
7 Forrester, "How Enterprise Smart Glasses Will Drive Workforce Enablement," https://www.forrester.com/report/How+Enterprise+Smart+Glasses+Will+Dr ive+Workforce+Enablement/-/E-RES133722.

moment transaction that is happening while you are engaged in an Augmented Reality, powered by Hyperconvergence.

NASA Explores How
We Will Work with AR in 2025

James Rinaldi, the CIO of JPL (Jet Propulsion Laboratory), has embarked on an initiative with the CIO of NASA called "Workplace 2025" to collaboratively predict, envision, and plan for how the organizations will work in the years ahead. NASA sees its future workplace as a much more immersive, augmented, and virtual environment: 3D printing and consumer robotics will be cheap and plentiful, space will be commercialized as NASA partners with private companies, and AR will be everywhere via apps, glasses, and wearable computing. Employees will wear data interfaces integrated into their clothes or glasses. And the organization will act more like a startup, as people will be able to work wherever data is available. Their work stations, which might be at their homes, will be a combination of extreme-resolution wall and head- and eye-mounted displays, which will create 3D visual environments. NASA imagines it will be a digitally enabled blend of real-world and virtual-world work environments, which could allow scientists, researchers, and engineers around the world to work together in real time in a way that is mobile, secure, automated, and integrated.

Prototypes for things such as engines will be analyzed in projected, touchable holography before being sent to automated fabrication teams. Brainstorming sessions and executive meetings will mix virtual and physical models, regardless of where workers are located, and the data/information will be shared everywhere at once, in a meaningful way. And getting the latest technologies into NASA missions will be easier because of rapid prototyping through 3D printing and visual programming and modeling.[8]

Something to consider for all future workplaces: these wearables and glasses will be more than *just* devices. They will receive information that helps enable interactions in the real world through analytics and sensors, ultimately helping us to work more efficiently and produce quality work in less time.

If things work out as JPL and NASA are predicting, why would we even need to leave the house? We could walk into our workspace every day in our own homes, or perhaps in a local or rental office space that we would share, near where we live. Or, potentially, each neighborhood could just have such a building, where people go in and attend their meetings, all around the world, for any organization. That is the direction we are moving in, and that kind of support

---

8 "How Will We Work in 2025?" NASA *IT Talk*, July-September 2014, https://www.nasa.gov/sites/default/files/files/IT-Talk_July2014.pdf.

infrastructure, with advanced technology, is really the basis of the theory of these *Transboundary Communities* (which we will learn more about later). Such communities will simulate in-person interactions but do so in a completely virtual way across vast distances.

Companies Testing AR

Augmented Reality is driving a new and different relationship with technology. Along with Hyperconvergence and Digital Moments, AR is another pillar of the new world of Singularity. When we talk about Digital Singularity and how it will affect the human experience, one of the overarching themes is how it will directly improve our visual and intellectual experience and context. Those benefits provide a significant amount of value. There are potential applications for AR in every vertical, from medical to manufacturing to telecommunications. But we are now just scratching the surface in terms of what is possible using AR.

Amazon has been innovating in a number of areas, expanding its technical prowess to grow its network of *physical* locations—beyond a few bookstores in Chicago and cashier-free grocery stores in Seattle. What is next: Augmented Reality furniture stores. The company is exploring the idea of opening stores that sell furniture and appliances with the aid of AR. How will it work? You would be able to use AR to see how couches, refrigerators, stoves, and credenzas will look in your house before you buy.[9] Some consumers have been hesitant to buy such large items sight unseen over the internet. Such a move will personalize the product for the buyer. AR applications also have the benefit of potentially increasing conversion (sales) rates by removing uncertainties that plague customers when shopping online or in stores when it is difficult to visualize how the product would look in your home.[10] The stores would become showcases where consumers could see the merchandise before it is delivered. Such a move could force the hand of rivals to try the same thing.[11]

There is another area where AR could improve efficiency and change the way we do business: warehouse distribution systems and supply chains. Freight company DHL is testing AR to bring down warehouse labor costs by streamlining and perfecting the process of selecting items ordered by customers

9 Jon Fingas, "Amazon Considers Opening Augmented Reality Furniture Stores," Engadget, March 26, 2017, https://www.engadget.com/2017/03/26/amazon-furniture-and-electronics-stores/.

10 Karl Siebrecht, "How Augmented Reality and Apple Will Transform Retail & Logistics Supply Chains," Supply Chain 24/7, June 26, 2017, http://www.supplychain247.com/article/how_augmented_reality_and_apple_will_transform_retail_logistics.

11 Nick Wingfield, "Amazon's Ambitions Unboxed: Stores for Furniture, Appliances and More," *New York Times,* March 25, 2017, https://www.nytimes.com/2017/03/25/technology/amazon-wants-to-crush-your-store-with-its-technology-might.html?_r=0.

from the inventory.[12] Augmented Reality could help empower warehouse staffs to not only identify goods on the shelf but to recognize whether they are in the right or wrong place, just by looking at them. Workers would be able to scan an entire warehouse and see where the red dots pop up on the visual scan to find items that have been misplaced and need to be relocated. The technology also confirms the correct product through optical readers that scan bar codes.[13] Soon enough, you may only need one person to run a warehouse of 100,000 square feet because technology will virtually identify all products that are out of place in mere seconds.

AR technology could be an asset for smaller businesses as well. Deli workers could simply look into their stockroom and their glasses would "tell" them to reorder rye bread because the technology would analyze the inventory and realize that there was a shortage. Workers would then be able to optimize the deli's supply chain and eventually automate ordering directly from the AR environment. By combining physical and digital views of the world, AR technology would allow them to run

12 Jennifer McKevitt and Kate Patrick, "Automation in Warehouses May Produce Higher ROI," Supply Chain Dive, July 17, 2017, https://www.supplychaindive.coJm/news/automation-artificial-intelligence-augmented-reality-DHL-Amazon/447181/.
13 Kristi Montgomery, "Why Use Augmented Reality in Your Warehouse or DC?" Talking Logistics, January 26, 2016, https://talkinglogistics.com/2016/01/26/why-use-augmented-reality-in-your-warehouse-or-dc/.

analytics in the stockroom, and even make it possible to measure how many slices of bread remained by taking a picture of it. The analytics from the glasses could support workers on the floor to make decisions that would support the overall strategy of the business. This is where the technology is headed.

Google is also working with Augmented Reality, hoping to turn your Android smartphone into an AR engine. Its Tango and ARCore platforms aim to bring Augmented Reality to millions of emerging and existing phones for apps and games. While Tango requires special cameras and sensors to 3D-map an environment,[14] ARCore works without any additional hardware and can pinpoint indoor locations and identify streets and buildings. It could ultimately also help find instructions for a machine after the user takes a picture of the object. Google hopes to make the technology available to app and software developers to grow the smartphone AR field[15] and eventually design it into smart glasses to replace your phone.[16]

---

14 Adi Robertson, "Google Arcore Gives Android Users Augmented Reality Without Tango," The Verge, August 29, 2017, https://www.theverge.com/2017/8/29/16219696/google-arcore-augmented-reality-platform-announce-release-pixel-samsung.

15 Robertson, "Google Arcore."

16 Steve Kovach, "Google's Augmented Reality Project Is the Coolest Thing It Showed Off This Week," Business Insider, May 29, 2017, http://www.businessinsider.com/google-tango-2017-5/#tango-is-cool-but-still-has-a-long-way-to-go-11.

Competition You Cannot "See"

Augmented Reality is already employed by different companies and verticals, but where it is moving is quite exciting.

- The hospitality industry will undergo a major change not just in terms of how customer service is provided but also how consumers are recognized and consume services. For example, instead of a front desk person checking people in, guests will bypass the desk, be scanned (with their prior approval), and be directed to their room by lighted pathway. This technology already exists and is beginning to be implemented. Another example: IBM has worked with Pebble Beach to create a virtual concierge app that provides customers with suggestions for exploration, restaurants, and experiences as they are driving, like having a tour guide traveling with them. The app serves up immersive AR experiences around those destinations, without the need for a concierge, and users can ask the app questions and get answers in real time.[17]

- In the utilities field, we can combine 3D imaging, sensors, and AR to spot outages and improve energy

---

17 Stephen Hennessy, "Pebble Beach Partners with IBM to Develop New App with Virtual Concierge," *Golf Digest, May 9, 2017,* https://www.golfdigest. com/story/pebble-beach-partners-with-ibm-to-develop-new-app-with-virtual-concierge.

and operational efficiency. Essentially, the grid could be replicated via AR glasses, which would display exact locations of outages and energy issues, along with a rating of how serious the problem is so that utility providers could prioritize repairs.

- The auto industry, thanks to connected cars, will simplify diagnoses of car troubles. You will get a diagnostic directly, and the problem will be resolved efficiently. You will get a communication: "There is something wrong with your car. Take it to a certified dealer. Here is a $25 coupon."

- In medicine, AR will assist in surgery. The technology will overlay a schematic of the heart as the doctor starts an angioplasty, or even a heart transplant. The surgeon will see every part of the organ, and will not just be relying on the visual but also on a representation of the heart that is overlaid on the actual heart.

As an executive or business owner, can you really afford not to start investing in Augmented Reality, or in any of the pillars? Remember, you have invisible competition you never could have imagined. The companies that are disrupting traditional businesses are not ones that we would expect. Amazon is a technology company—make no mistake. Uber is a technology company that is competing with taxi drivers and limo drivers. The new disruptive companies may not even be on your radar yet.

But this is an opportunity for businesses to embrace. If you think about Clayton Christensen's concept of disruption, disruptive innovation is natural—it is like breathing. If there is a chance to make something more efficient and less expensive, human beings will find a way to do just that. And, in this time of rapid change happening right before our eyes, we will need every advantage to stay ahead of the curve.

CHAPTER SEVEN

DIGITAL TWINS: COMBINING PHYSICAL AND VIRTUAL ENTITIES INTO INTEGRATED ACTIONS

Some very large cyberattacks have occurred in recent years. In fact, Symantec Corp.'s 2016 Internet Security Threat Report indicates that between 2011 and 2015, the percentage of spear-phishing attacks—more personalized, targeted attempts to steal sensitive information—targeting small businesses jumped from 18 percent to 43 percent, and that number continues to grow exponentially. This is not just a trend but a reality of the new economy. Businesses will need to better protect themselves and invest in advanced technologies to ensure more secure transactions.

The 2017 breach of the credit agency Equifax affected more than 140 million people and hundreds of thousands of credit and debit cards.[1] Yahoo has been hit twice, with hackers making off with the personal information of nearly 1 billion users[2]—including not only encrypted passwords but the security questions to reset them. In the first half of 2017 alone nearly 1.9 billion records were compromised, up 164 percent from the same period a year prior—and nine billion records have been exposed since 2013.[3] Hackers even gained access into the National Security Agency and are now selling NSA cyberweapons to countries hostile to the U.S.[4] The number and intricacy of the attacks will only increase.

---

1 Michael Hiltzik, "Here Are All the Ways the Equifax Data Breach Is Worse Than You Can Imagine," *Los Angeles Times,* September 8, 2017, http://www. latimes.com/business/hiltzik/la-fi-hiltzik-equifax-breach-20170908-story.html.
2 Vindu Goel and Nicole Perlroth, "Yahoo Says 1 Billion User Accounts Were Hacked," *New York Times,* December 14, 2016, https://www.nytimes. com/2016/12/14/technology/yahoo-hack.html.
3 Nichole Perlroth, "All 3 Billion Yahoo Accounts Were Affected by 2013 Attack," *New York Times, October 3, 2017,* https://www.nytimes. com/2017/10/03/technology/yahoo-hack-3-billion-users.html?mtrref=www. google.com&gwh=89422209A8BF9A29C0B32AF97F1CAF93&gwt=pay.
4 Scott Shane, Nichole Perlroth, and David E. Sanger, "Security Breach and Spilled Secrets Have Shaken the N.S.A. to Its Core," *New York Times,* November 12, 2017, https://www.nytimes.com/2017/11/12/us/nsa-shadow-brokers.html?utm_source=newsletter&utm_medium=email&utm_campaign=newsletter_axiosam&stream=top-stories&_r=0&mtrref=undefined.

While we may want to simply disconnect and go live in the woods in light of the many attacks, one thing is clear: Your information is already online. The truth is we are now living in the digital world, and much of our data is insecure. So, what can we do? What if there were a way to lock everything digital that we hold dear?

We are moving in that direction now, and soon enough we will resolve the challenge of automating our daily activities and simultaneously protecting our data. What we are talking about is what we call *Digital Twins*, a real-time, virtual model of our physical selves that is constantly transacting and acting on our behalf through automation—without ever needing to rest or refuel. The digital twin will only be accessed via biometrics and will be programmed to protect our vital information.

Although we cannot ultimately stop all hacks or criminals, our digital twin will be our online persona, managing all of our data and continuously working to secure our identity from cyberattacks. Imagine having the power to program the digital twin to change the passwords of all of our online accounts every thirty minutes. By consolidating our personal information with our digital twin, we permit it to conduct transactions for us and secure all of our digital assets and records as never before.

While some may hesitate to share their financial, health, and personal data with their digital twin, consider that many felt the same about banking institutions before they were backed by governments and insurance policies.

As the digital economy makes large investments in cyber-security and other Technology Prerequisites like blockchain, cloud, and artificial intelligence, the digital twin will continue to advance in security and efficiency. Our twin will become the lockbox for seven aspects of our physical and digital lives:

- relationship management
- financial management
- security management
- social communities we belong to
- work and school lives
- purchasing transactions
- health

The way we are defining Digital Twins goes beyond the current definition you may have seen online. Some people consider a digital twin to be a virtual rendition of a physical object or process that helps analyze and stop problems before they occur.[5] We define Digital Twins as a complete transactional, real-time approximation of all knowledge and action that physical entities, like us, can possess or conduct. And these

---

5 Bernard Marr, "What Is Digital Twin Technology—and Why Is It So Important?" *Forbes,* March 6, 1017, https://www.forbes.com/sites/bernardmarr/2017/03/06/what-is-digital-twin-technology-and-why-is-it-so-important/#24ba6a882e2a.

transactions are not only about buying and selling products; they are also communications with our family members, friends, and associates, like remembering someone's birthday with well wishes. In essence, we are giving *something*, material or intangible, and getting something back.

But a digital twin is not a Google search tool, an engine used to explore data that exists online. It is an extension of our being. It *is* us. It is our identity as we want to be perceived, physically and electronically, and it is safe. Some people may mistake the digital twin for being our *physical* robot—it is not. It is actually our own electronic persona, our virtual public face.

As we move toward a world where more transactions are happening electronically, the digital twin will be able to keep up with those transactions and even accelerate them at a pace that a human could not. The digital twin makes use of robotic process automation—a currently available technology and one of our Digital Singularity Technology Prerequisites—to automate our human activities and processes that would otherwise have to be done manually. Since Digital Twins are one of our four pillars, other Technology Prerequisites like cybersecurity and artificial intelligence will also be critical for our digital twin to function, as it protects us and performs tasks on our behalf. Without the prerequisites, we could not have the pillars or the rules for the new digital economy.

The Digital Twin: Our Protector and Security

In the future, we may be able to subscribe to a digital twin service or platform where we could buy modules to manage our personal, financial, and work lives. These modules would be preprogrammed to carry out activities, such as buying groceries, paying bills, balancing our checkbooks, or whatever else we may need. Need other services? Just download the app or configuration that will train the digital twin to "learn" how to do these for us. That platform, which will *be* our digital twin, might charge us on a monthly basis to secure and protect such things as our social security numbers and our passport information, and allow us to consolidate all of our information, as well as our data from our personal and professional lives.

Our digital twin will not only protect our vital information and records, it will also be able to alter and update the data that it maintains. And since it will have our retinal and facial scans and fingerprints, it will be able to assist us in a variety of ways throughout our daily lives, in ways like these:

- Balance our checkbook, manage our financial life, and provide transaction reports— all while checking for errors, fraud and potential identity theft.

- Maintain our social relationships by letting us know that we have not been in touch with a friend or client for too long, or that someone close to us personally or professionally is visiting our city, looking to buy something, or even planning a trip. The digital twin would also work to engage with our LinkedIn contacts and manage other relationships.

- Centrally manage our social media accounts, including postings and privacy settings. Our digital twin would be able to consolidate all of our information and privacy settings in one place, which will save time and increase security. With Digital Twins, personal data will be protected so we can avoid many threats we face today.

- Communicate with our doctors. When they ask for our health history, the digital twin could provide them with all the relevant information.

- File our taxes automatically with the IRS by pulling data from our bank and financial records.

Digital Twins will also do much more. They will become a regular part of our lives for security, banking, health, and shopping. Our digital twin will deliver the right authentication for every transaction because it will have all the necessary information. And best of all, we will *direct* the digital twin to do this. In other words, the digital twin is not a *sentient* being; it is not conscious or "alive." It will rely on machine learning and be absolutely under our control, and it will acquire more "intelligence" as AI advances. It will work under our direction, conducting thousands of transactions as we teach it to do more of what we want. And since we will control our digital twin, it will shop around for the best deal and identify the top choices based upon our preferences. The transactions will happen automatically. If we are sleeping, the digital twin is searching online for us and looking out for our security; it is also buying and selling for us. Our digital twin will connect with the people around us and operate in the background ecosystem to make our lives safer, easier, and more efficient.

Our digital twin will even manage and protect us and our estate after we are no longer around. The digital twin has the potential to live beyond us, carrying out our wishes and the instructions of any trust we establish. Essentially, the digital twin would be certified and owned by the trust, with the authority to execute on our behalf. After a person's death, the trustee or surviving parent, child, or significant other could interact with the digital twin to handle the remaining estate. And, when the trustee needs access to all of our accounts and insurances, the digital twin could become managed by the trustee. The survivors could decide whether to continue to pay the subscription for the digital twin service to keep it going long after we are gone. In a way, the digital twin would enable us to live on, with access to all of our accounts and finances. It would be a truly timeless manifestation of ourselves and remain programmed to do what we wish.

Digital Twins are the last of the four pillars on our journey toward Singularity. In Chapter 4, we laid out how the four pillars come together to make Digital Singularity an opportunity for all. Our Digital Twins will make the transactions and actions of Digital Moments possible and allow us to interact in the ecosystem seamlessly. Digital Twins—along with Augmented Reality and hyperconverged technologies—represent a critical, connective technology and one of the building blocks required for us to progress to the new world of digital business.

Digital Twins and Security

We already live in a world where we provide sensitive information about our bank accounts, credit cards, and social security numbers to multiple organizations. The digital twin will encrypt all of that data to protect it from people who might use it against us. Today, it is very difficult to manage all our passwords and all of our activities online. When you have a digital twin, you will never again have to find a reliable way to remember your many passwords, like you do now: committing them to memory, writing them down, putting them on Evernote for safekeeping, or even using a password manager. As secure as we think we are, in reality we are not when using these methods—notes get lost, security flaws are revealed by hackers, and software can be vulnerable. Even our trusty Wi-Fi network protocols have been revealed to be open to attacks by mischievous eavesdroppers.[6]

Add to this the fact that many of us use very common names for passwords, and about 40 percent of us use the same password across many sites. Also, nearly a third of us have a hard time keeping track of our passwords and worry how secure they really are.[7] Soon enough, when we want to make a change, or we have been hacked, the digital twin will be able to manage it centrally for us. It will automatically connect to all of our financial, personal, professional, and social relationships. We will empower it with all the information that we already possess today, and enable it to learn even more with more powerful tools in the future. Companies that offer a digital twin service will likely comply with rigorous standards and reflect industrywide best practices.

As we have said, the digital twin will consolidate all of our passwords and personal data and allow us to protect them better. Consider that today we already do this when

6 Thomas Fox-Brewster, "Update Every Device—This KRACK Hack Kills Your Wi-Fi Privacy," *Forbes,* October 16, 2017, https://www.forbes.com/sites/thomasbrewster/2017/10/16/krack-attack-breaks-wifi-encryption/#48aa194c2ba9.

7 Kenneth Olmsted and Aaron Smith, "Password Management and Mobile Security," Pew Research Center, January 26, 2017, http://www.pewinternet.org/2017/01/26/2-password-management-and-mobile-security/.

we use cloud services and email, or when we put money in the bank. But while it may seem counterintuitive, we are more secure having everything together in *one* place than in a hundred places.

Heading Toward Digital Twins

Digital Twins will work well for finance and transactions—but our digital twin will do more than act as an antifraud tool. For example, doctors could use their digital twin to communicate regularly with patients, check on expiring prescriptions, transfer prescriptions to the pharmacy, invoice patients, and even schedule appointments. The digital twin is truly designed to eliminate human activities that are repetitive and even mundane. This will give people more time to focus on higher-value activities.

One of our hobbies might be exploring caves in exotic places. Our digital twin could help find the best cave for spelunking. The digital twin would know we like a certain level of difficulty—perhaps, water in the caves—and would research for us, through maps, "visit" each cave virtually, then suggest destinations we might like to visit. All the while, the digital twin is learning our preferences and likes, so it can make appropriate recommendations. Again, we still have full power over the digital twin, but we can authorize it to make informed choices and decisions, at our discretion.

We might not be at the spelunking stage just yet, but we are now taking very elementary steps toward making digital twin technology a reality and putting into action those things that are important to us. Let us look at some of the existing technologies a digital twin will actually employ:

- Fingerprint and facial recognition technologies are already used to unlock our phones. It is an innovative step forward, but these capabilities have not been integrated with other technologies to secure our identity and lives.

- Many people use Amazon's Alexa and Google Home digital assistants. But these devices' capabilities can seem fairly limited. For example, you can ask Alexa to order an Uber or a pizza, search for something online, or play a song. But there are shortcomings to its voice-interaction ability. You can use just one command at a time, as its knowledge to answer questions is a narrow set, and background noise undermines its ability to understand commands.[8] Also, there is no AI that connects to our financial lives, such as the ability to make recommendations for our portfolio, and the devices do not have access to the full aggregate of our data. These devices

---

8 Grant Clauser, "What Is Alexa? What Is the Amazon Echo, and Should You Get One?" *Wirecutter*, February 1, 2018, https://thewirecutter.com/reviews/what-is-alexa-what-is-the-amazon-echo-and-should-you-get-one/#alexas-limitations.

are crude prototypes for a working digital twin, but the innovative AI of an actual digital twin will likely make Alexa seem like a somewhat-smart walkie-talkie.

- Google's original product, its search tool, equips your browser with your preferences, bookmarks, and various features you like, no matter what computer you use. It customizes and configures your device's browser to act just like the one on your other devices, and it has stored all of your passwords. But this is only a digital twin at its most basic level. It lacks intelligence; it is really just a storehouse of your passwords and preferences.

While we still may be a long way from a properly functioning digital twin, the good thing is regulations already govern connection of our health, privacy, and data records. This is no longer the Wild West on the internet. Regulations always seem to catch up—as they did for taxing products bought over the internet—and regulation of the digital twin will be necessary. Like the Health Insurance Portability and Accountability Act (HIPAA), which provides data privacy and security requirements for keeping medical information safe, and the Federal Information Security Management Act (FISMA)—a framework to protect government information, assets, and operations—Digital Twins will need precise rules about authentication to ensure that transactions can occur.

As the technology advances, our digital twin will require underlying insurance to safeguard losses from security breaches, so we can be certain it is safe. The digital twin should help us manage hacking and also be programmed to notify authorities or shut down accounts if there is unexpected spending or activity. If there is a hack, our digital twin would be insured for losses. As Digital Twins become more possible and available, security companies will employ them to manage all of our digital assets, which, as we stated, are protected by questionable security.

Today, many homeowner insurance policies include an identity theft provision; this option has been around for more than ten years. So, the concept of insuring identity theft is well established on a foundational level. In the future, our Digital Twins will also be insured by large companies, and the insurance industry policies toward Digital Twins will mature accordingly as technology further develops in this area.

Some of the building blocks of Digital Twins are quickly coming into play. The problem is they are not yet sophisticated enough and are disconnected.

Digital Twins as an Advantage for Business

The cost to business from digital fraud has been steadily climbing, which has led to a number of challenges. The cost per dollar of e-commerce fraud grew 9 percent from 2015 to 2016. Mobile commerce hit 12 percent. What about in-store? We are looking at just 3 percent. All of this leads to lost revenue.[9]

Huge numbers—trillions of dollars—are also lost in leakage through illegal transactions online, despite U.S. and European authorities bringing down two of the biggest online black markets, AlphaBay and Hansa Market, in 2017.[10] Lowering the high cost of fraud will be a necessity if we are going to live in the digital reality.

The good news is that Digital Twins' authentication and security capabilities will be essential for wiping out, regulating, and managing such fraud and attacks. Twins could soon work to secure transactions and become effective marketing channels for companies and retailers to reach consumers.

In the near future, a digital twin will be the primary channel for selling products, services, and financial packages. It will become the channel by which people buy, well, everything. With the digital twin, we can automate both business

9 "Rising Digital Fraud Presents New Challenges," Business Insider, June 1, 2016, http://www.businessinsider.com/rising-digital-fraud-presents-new-challenges-2016-5.
10 Nathaniel Popper and Rebecca R. Ruiz, "2 Leading Online Black Markets Are Shut Down by Authorities," *New York Times,* July 20, 2017, https://www.nytimes.com/2017/07/20/business/dealbook/alphabay-dark-web-opioids.html.

and personal activities, which will free up our time. We will have more time to explore new business innovation. Our twin will not just buy goods; it will buy time with our families and friends, and it will be part of all our activities.

If this is how consumers are going to buy, interact in social networks, and engage in Digital Moments and financial transactions, whether you are a bank, a retailer, or a service industry—you now have the potential to market *to* the digital twin. What does that mean?

Our digital twin will be able to react automatically to advertisements and offers. Essentially, the digital twin will have the authority to create hundreds of transactions a second for us, which will give businesses instant and ready access to "us" via the digital twin. This is a tremendous advantage to business, because the digital twin will always be "listening." With all the information and noise, we just do not seem to have the time nor the ability to analyze an infinite number of transactions—but the digital twin does. Think about your digital twin on "Black Friday": it will always look for the best deal, best price, and best way to get it soon.

Through machine learning, the digital twin will interpret our preferences and anticipate our needs. Much of this is yet to be realized, but it is certainly within the realm of possibility and expectation. For example, the digital twin could take advantage of interest and account promotions from banks. It could distribute money across our accounts and remind us that we need to open a new account, then research the best options based upon the banks we patronize.

This will result in a huge efficiency advantage, both for consumers and clients. It is the kind of capability that illustrates why companies that fail to learn about Digital Twins will be missing a part of the market that will be interacting with companies in a new way. It will become the price of admission for doing business.

To continue the kind of incredible growth in online transactions that we will soon see, we will need Digital Twins in place. Twins will provide security for businesses, which are paying higher levels of insurance—and we all pay for fraud.

CHAPTER EIGHT

ACCESS, COMPETITION, AND SHARING LIKE NEVER BEFORE

We have spent some time talking about the four pillars—technologies existing or emerging whose presence signals the onset of Digital Singularity. So, how will Hyperconvergence, Augmented Reality, Digital Moments, and Digital Twins change our lives in the near future? Together, these technology pillars will allow us to experience the new world in new ways.

In this chapter, we will be exploring the final, inner circle of the core elements of the digital economy rubric that will signal the onset of Digital Singularity. Remember that the Technology Prerequisites, the basic technologies needed to even live in the digital world, form the foundation for the next layer, the Four Pillars of Digital Singularity, which in turn create new platforms for commerce and social interaction. The Rules of the New Economy, the final level, show us how Digital Singularity will function. In this new world, the rules will have changed and individuals will experience Barrier-free Access, Democratized Egalitarianism, The Sharing Economy, and Transboundary Communities. These are the elements that define a digital economy.

When we are deeply connected to the cloud and to each other, personally and professionally, the Rules of the New Economy drive the technologies that bring us closer together, instead of splitting us apart. They also build the social construct for how we share and consume information and data, how we work and play, how we share our lives with others across the globe, and how we buy and sell everything. The first step involves getting access to information.

Barrier-free Access and Democratized Egalitarianism

When we have *Barrier-free Access*, we have the totality of information at our fingertips, regardless of our social status or level of wealth. And that means we have direct access to the global economy.

Today, information is largely available to many people for free. When everyone has access to the internet in the future, no longer will access to information be a benefit only for the

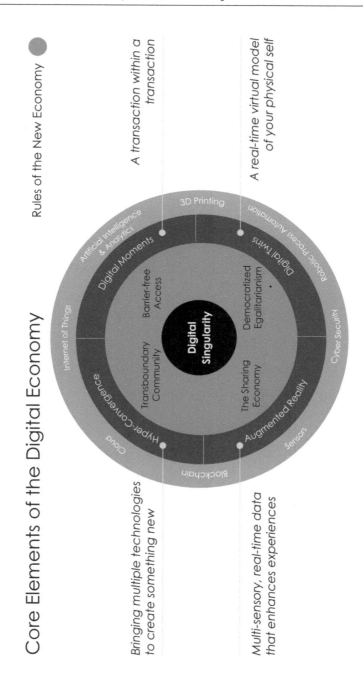

Core Elements of the Digital Economy

Rules of the New Economy

A transaction within a transaction

A real-time virtual model of your physical self

3D Printing

Artificial Intelligence & Analytics

Digital Moments

Barrier-free Access

Robotic Process Automation

Digital Twins

Internet of Things

Democratized Egalitarianism

Digital Singularity

Transboundary Community

The Sharing Economy

Cyber Security

Hyper-Convergence

Augmented Reality

Cloud

Sensors

Blockchain

Bringing multiple technologies to create something new

Multi-sensory, real-time data that enhances experiences

privileged. The internet will allow for this, and connect us to everything online, with instant gratification. We will all have the same access to many types of information, and we will all able to find the *same* information—whether you are an executive or an assistant, a factory worker or a factory owner. When we have the same access, we will be able to play outside established rules. This leveling of the playing field will provide immense advancement opportunities for education and jobs. We are starting to see glimpses of this now.

Historically, life for many of us proceeded like this: attend a four-year college, study hard, learn a lot, get mentored by someone, go to work for a big company, stay there for forty years, and retire. Today, we can follow a different path. We can become sought-after experts ourselves quickly through new, unconventional paths to employment.

Increasingly, having access to information is critical for getting an education. With the internet, learning no longer requires sitting in a classroom. Nontraditional education—including online classes, universities, and accredited degrees—is on the rise. About three-quarters of college administrators said there has been an increase in demand for online courses at their institutions.[1] And nearly two-thirds of all

---

1 BestColleges.com, "2017 Online Colleges Trend Report," http://www. bestcolleges.com/wp-content/uploads/2017-Online-Education-Trends-Report.pdf.

colleges reported that their distance (online) education enrollments grew from 2012 to 2015.[2]

Amid higher fees and other concerns, skepticism about the value of a traditional four-year degree is growing among those who do not have one: just 49 percent of young adults believe a college degree will lead them toward a good job and higher earnings, while 47 percent do not, according to a *Wall Street Journal*/NBC News survey.[3]

The surge of more affordable and IT-focused online education programs known as nanodegrees is bringing into question the whole idea of a more traditional education route and is, instead, giving people new options for careers that are more aligned with industry needs. More people are asking: *If going to a university for four years to compete in the new digital economy is not necessarily required to get a high-paying job, why do it?* For less than a fraction of what colleges cost, and in much less time, people are going to online education providers like Udacity and Coursera to earn certifications in skill sets that will likely become more and more crucial to earning a living as we sprint toward Singularity. Udacity is offering courses,

---

2 Digital Learning Compass, "Distance Education Enrollment Report 2017," http://digitallearningcompass.org/.
3 Josh Mitchell and Doug Belkin, "Americans Losing Faith in College Degrees, Poll Finds," *Wall Street Journal*, September 7, 2017, https://www.wsj.com/articles/americans-losing-faith-in-college-degrees-poll-finds-1504776601.

and degree programs, for people to become self-driving-car engineers, data analysts, VR developers, and even artificial intelligence engineers. And tech employers are more readily accepting the degrees as legitimate entryways into specialized jobs. One of the online providers' programs even promises that students will get a job within six months of earning their degree, or they get their money back.

As we are seeing, there are many possibilities and new paths to jobs, and the market for this activity is only growing. Now, we can take online courses at an online university, maybe occasionally attend a class in person, work our own hours as an Uber or Lyft driver to supplement income, start a business at home, study to become a social media or search engine optimization expert, or even build a following as an Instagram model or influencer and make, potentially, $150,000 or more a year.

Having all of this access has given rise to the "gig economy," meaning the legions of freelancers, contractors, and temporary employees working outside the traditional system in many different jobs, social-oriented and otherwise. The number of Americans who are self-employed is increasing each year.[4] By 2020, more than 40 percent of

4 Bureau of Labor Statistics, "Selected Economic Indicators," press release, https://www.bls.gov/news.release/empsit.t09.htm.

the U.S. workforce will be independent workers.[5] While independent contractors may not have the security of a fixed salary or benefits like healthcare or a 401(k), they enjoy a great deal of freedom.

Barrier-free Access means we do not have to be special or advantaged in some way to get ahead; we just need to be industrious to create opportunities for ourselves in unconventional job and education markets. If we are all able to use the same information and data, then we are effectively equal in many respects. This brings up the second concept driving innovative technologies: *Democratized Egalitarianism*, the ability of technology to further and drive the equality of all voices. It is a big megaphone that allows us to be heard, regardless of where, or who, we are.

Democratized Egalitarianism extends the concept of Barrier-free Access to the role people will play in government and society. Today, we are starting to see how our connectivity gives us all a voice with the same power and resonance. People who are less privileged can directly declare their opinions about the government and garner attention for their ideas and beliefs just as easily as those with more disposable income

---

5 Intuit, "Twenty Trends That Will Shape the Next Decade," http://httpdownload.intuit.com/http.intuit/CMO/intuit/futureofsmallbusiness/intuit_2020_report.pdf.

can—whether it is football quarterback Colin Kaepernick protesting the treatment of minorities, a consumer complaining about an experience at the DMV, or a user tweeting directly to the president of the United States.

Democratized Egalitarianism and Barrier-free Access will give everyone the opportunity to participate in the digital economy. It will provide a voice for all individuals. Everyone can work, conduct commerce, and have a say in this global economy. We already have the beginnings of a technology infrastructure readily available to empower people to compete with anyone in the world.

Across the globe, people have more opportunity and chances to start businesses that may not have been possible in their geographical locations before. Through the possibilities of the digital world, we can carry out whatever business and projects we want. We can be anywhere in the world and be part of the global economy.

One example of how this is currently working is via a new service called Amazon Mechanical Turk: More than 500,000 workers in 190 countries are selling their time in microminutes. Companies can hire multiple workers with specialized skills for less time and cost than was previously thought possible. Silicon Valley has taken notice, hiring some workers to perform tasks like writing code or AI algorithms, or creating Google

Chrome plug-ins—and there is also a forum where workers can ask each other for advice.[6]

There are many gig platforms, such as TaskRabbit, Upwork, and PeoplePerHour, to choose from, and the number of companies has been growing over the past few years. Fortune 500 companies interested in more flexible, lower-cost ways to hire are increasingly turning to these platforms to find workers with specialized knowledge.

These platforms provide additional ways for people to make money and supplement their income through a newfound sense of freedom. For many freelancers this is not just a side job; they are not just dabbling, they are in it for the long haul. In a recent study, two-thirds said they plan on freelancing for ten or more years, and 65 percent said they believe their lives as freelancers have been improving.[7]

The Sharing Economy

When we have equal access to the digital economy and a virtual bullhorn to amplify our voices across the globe, this

---

6 Miranda Katz, "Amazon's Turker Crowed Has Had Enough," *Wired*, August 23, 2017, https://www.wired.com/story/amazons-turker-crowd-has-had-enough/.

7 Jordan Teicher, "The State of Freelancing 2015," Contently, June 22, 2015, http://contently.net/2015/06/22/resources/contently-study-state-freelancing-2015/.

brings up the third concept that helps establish the rules for the Digital Age: *The Sharing Economy*. It is how we can offer our services to the world.

Whereas in the twentieth century, amassing objects—cars, homes, possessions of every size and shape—was a sign of success, we are now owning less and sharing more: rides, residences, and even work. The Sharing Economy puts an economic spin on this idea and is a model of providing and acquiring goods and services aided by a collaborative, community-based technology platform. The Sharing Economy brings resources from around the world together to build and deliver products and services, relying on Transboundary Communities as well as the concepts of Barrier-free Access and Democratized Egalitarianism.

Clothing retailers and car companies, which traditionally have focused on selling and ownership, are now exploring options for renting and subscriptions. Consumers and sellers are beginning to value access, convenience, and experiences over ownership.[8] Rent the Runway, Bag Borrow Steal, Chic by Choice, and a number of others are helping change the way we view and obtain clothing and accessories, stressing renting

---

8 Brooke Masters, "Winners and Losers in The Sharing Economy," *Financial Times,* December 28, 2017, https://www.ft.com/content/c97eaa72-eaf8-11e7-bd17-521324c81e23.

and borrowing instead of buying outright. Need a dress for a special occasion? Rent one online, or get a subscription, and change your wardrobe every month.

Now that you have your outfit, do you need to get across town for a meeting? Peer-to-peer car sharing site Getaround and local-hosts rental company Turo will get you a car fast and within the means of any budget. Even long-established car companies are getting into the game to service those not looking for a long-term commitment. Cadillac recently launched a luxury car subscription service: For $1,500 a month, you can reserve a car via app, and registration, insurance, and maintenance are included. Porsche and Volvo have also launched subscription programs.[9]

Need something simpler, like a bicycle? Even that mode of transportation has become part of The Sharing Economy, providing a way to get from place to place or connecting people to public transportation. Cities around the world have bike racks that offer rentable two-wheelers for short trips. More recently, multiple dockless bike-share companies have allowed commuters to rent a bike and leave it at their final destination. China's version of this bike service, which did not

---

9 E.J. Schultz, "Netflix for Cars? Cadillac Launches Subscription Service," *Ad Age*, January 5, 2017, http://adage.com/article/cmo-strategy/netflix-cars-cadillac-launches-subscription-service/307373/.

exist three years ago, has now swelled to include more than forty companies, two of which handle more than fifty million riders a day. In 2016, China's sharing economy drummed up $500 billion in transactions from approximately six hundred million people. It is expected to account for 20 percent of the country's GDP by 2025.[10]

What Makes Sharing Work: Transboundary Communities

When we have equal access—regardless of where we live or our economic means—the same voice, and the ability to work how and when we want, we can all be a part of this digital economy. The last rule of the new economy is *Transboundary Communities*, which make The Sharing Economy function as it should. Transboundary Communities occur when digital communication platforms become an avenue for people of like minds and interests to interact. Transboundary Communities occur when people collaborate to accomplish new things, all while competing for business with other individuals or even with other companies on the same level. Transboundary Communities, which we call "designer worlds," allow us to connect and communicate with those close to us, regardless

---

10 Brook Larmer, "China's Revealing Spin on the 'Sharing Economy,'" *New York Times,* November 5, 2017, https://www.nytimes.com/2017/11/20/magazine/chinas-revealing-spin-on-the-sharing-economy.html.

of geography, using various technologies to build our own reality of the world around us.

Transboundary Communities exist now and will continue to advance as technology evolves. They do and will feature augmented human interactions as well as the ability to communicate with people in real time, tapping into multiple senses, to provide a richer communication experience. Traditionally, with the telephone, we have been limited to the single sense of hearing to drive our interactions. As we move to more immersive interactions, we will use real-time video and other sensory-driven technologies for a multisensory experience. As opposed to the linear communications we have with the Facebook communities we are familiar with—your friend posts a photo, you "like" it, she responds with the comment, "Thank you!"—a Transboundary Community experience is more intuitive and allows people to have a comprehensive way of communicating with each other.

A Transboundary Community has two specific elements: 1) it happens in real time, in a nonlinear fashion, and 2) it involves two or more of the five senses, as opposed to other technologies we have used in the past. In a Transboundary Community, we can capture the moments within the conversation, share documents and ideas visually, and cultivate and develop relationships through a more engaged way of connecting. It also could include Augmented Reality or sensory experiences to socialize, meet people, and do our work. Transboundary Communities can exist at work, home, and everywhere in between.

These communities are the equivalent of our neighbors in our own small-town versions of Mayberry, the fictitious community that was the setting for *The Andy Griffith Show*. But towns like Mayberry are rare. Why? We have become disconnected from our neighbors, and yet more connected to the rest of the world through the internet. Our face-to-face conversations have been replaced by virtual chat rooms and the myriad social platforms that we spend hours on every day.

We now have an opportunity to rebuild the quality of relationships that we have lost over the last decade and beyond—and Transboundary Communities will give us back some of that contact. Mayberry now only comes to life in a virtual way when we communicate with like-minded people. We consume information in a Transboundary Community that is curated around what we believe and value. We "design" the people and communities that we want to be around. We keep liking them on social media, they keep liking us, Facebook continues to suggest content that aligns with our value structure, and we keep building a social reality.

An interesting example of a Transboundary Community is Nextdoor, a social application intent on reestablishing a nationwide network of private neighborhoods. In other words, it connects neighbors. Now, it is using technology to get people back together again to share information about what is happening in town, in the church group, the book club, or in whatever else that matters most. Individuals do that by forming their own social communities that may be virtual but are very real.

Neighbors in Sarasota, Florida, recently came to understand Nextdoor's premise: it was formed on the idea that the neighborhood is a vital and useful community in a person's life. As Hurricane Irma approached Florida in 2017, neighbors before and after the disaster reached out to each other with messages asking for extra generators, reports of sparking telephone poles, requests for help filling sandbags and removing debris, and spreading up-to-date news. Nextdoor has become an invaluable way for neighbors to share news and alert each other in times of need. It also helps local residents plan social activities, like setting up a homegrown music festival, when the weather is more cooperative.[11]

But The Sharing Economy and the Transboundary Communities within it are not just about providing information

---

11 Ilene Denton, "Social Media App Nextdoor Kept Neighbors Connected During Hurricane Irma," *Sarasota,* September 14, 2017, https://www.sarasotamagazine.com/articles/2017/9/14/nextdoor-app-hurricane-irma-sarasota.

and procuring vehicles and clothes—they are about new types of workplaces that are fueling an "economy of one," in which individuals decide how to allocate their time and talents to earn a living, work with others, compete, and start new businesses. People can offer skills and experiences that may or may not be compensated, and they contribute and share knowledge. An example of such a community would be the organization HitRecord, an online company owned and directed by actor Joseph Gordon-Levitt, where artists collaborate on music, video, or book projects. Anyone with an internet connection can contribute. The people involved do not physically meet each other, but they are all working together, adding their own creative know-how to the project during their free time. The best collaborative efforts are developed for sale and distribution, with everyone sharing in the royalties. Perhaps, soon enough, they will be paid in cryptocurrencies due to the multijurisdictional nature of the work.

Many businesses are already leveraging collaborative sharing of talents. When firms want a new logo, they can work with companies like 99designs, an online graphic design marketplace. Clients have a quick conference to tell the company what they are thinking of, then 99designs launches a design contest within its community of one million professional designers. The firm will then receive dozens of designs, give feedback, and choose the winner. Instead of following the traditional route of going to a marketing agency and dealing with branding experts and strategies—all of which takes a lot of time and money—they can leverage the power of The Sharing Economy. A number of artists and designers, who normally work at some of the top marketing firms in the world, are now empowered to compete on the same playing field. They are able to offer services directly to the marketplace, without a company or a team behind them. The result? Great work for only a few hundred dollars, instead of tens of thousands.

Where Transboundary Communities Are Headed

In the near future, Transboundary Communities will be omnipresent, meaning they will always be on. They will function with enhanced wearables, sensor technology, and cognitive technologies, and will be driven by user experience. Transboundary Communities will be virtual communities, but provide a real-world experience in real time, where the digital and physical converge. In this community, you might put on your AR goggles and interact with people at that very moment. Instead of merely "talking" to the family, as on a conference call, you could have another experience altogether. When family members join up online, they can have a sensory experience: Mom gives a "hug," and you get optical and haptic feedback—sensations from vibrating actuators and waveform patterns sent to the user to convey information—through a sensor that simulates the touch. You will feel like you are all really *there*.

We are starting to see this technology at work by companies like Polycom and Cisco, whose immersive platforms enable real-time interactions with people who could be next door or five time zones away from us. They are hitting the market in varying levels of sophistication. Cisco's TelePresence and Polycom's RealPresence technologies create interactive, real-time meetings. Participants collaborate via large high-definition video screens, along with 4k cameras and theater-quality audio.[12] The audiovisual components come together to form a boardroom conference table in one room that is perfectly aligned and connected to the table of the other people in the meeting, who could be at an office somewhere else in the world. Participants see everyone sitting down at the same table in the same room, which provides a very connected experience. This technology will only advance in the workplace in the future.

In addition, a new application by Facebook called Workplace is designed to create a more "live" experience with at-the-moment

---

12 Cisco product information, https://www.cisco.com/c/en/us/products/collaboration-endpoints/ix5000-series/index.html#~stickynav=1; Polycom product information, http://www.polycom.com/products-services/hd-telepresence-video-conferencing/realpresence-immersive/realpresence-immersive-studio.html.

video, messaging, and collaboration.[13] This is just the beginning: we will soon merge sensor technology with wearables to create nonlinear experiences featuring virtual whiteboards and people potentially showing up holographically in each of the chairs.

The Digital Enterprise and Putting the Customer First

With The Sharing Economy on the rise and Transboundary Communities emerging, there is a real opportunity for enterprises. Why? We will have to build products and solutions that will appeal to these communities, and we will have to find ways to reach out to them. To succeed in this new economy, companies will need to understand how to function as a digital enterprise.

A digital enterprise understands this new human renaissance we are moving steadily toward. It puts the customer first and works to tailor products directly for them. It is clear that we are moving from a manufacturing-based economy to one driven by customer demand and enabled by technology. In this new digital economy, individuals tell us what, how, and when they want the product, and we deliver it to them directly.

The traditional value chain for an enterprise moves at analog speed and puts the customer last. The product begins

---

13 Facebook Workplace information, https://www.facebook.com/workplace.

with the supplier's raw materials and travels to manufacturing, the warehouse, the distribution system, the retailer, and then to the customer. The digital enterprise value chain moves at the speed of technology and starts with the individual. Individuals—customers or business owners—detail what they want, the product and solution is customized to their needs, and a profile is generated detailing their likes and dislikes. A product is then built, and it gets delivered to their home or business. It is a highly personalized experience.

We have discussed examples of this with fashion box companies like Trendy Butler and Stitch Fix, which style, choose, and deliver clothes as part of a monthly subscription. A stylist customizes clothes just for you, and if you do not like them, you can send them back; the club adjusts your portfolio as it learns what you like and dislike. The company will send you clothes every month that are appropriate for your body, modern, and stylish. This is what the best digital enterprises do: begin and end with the individual and what that individual desires.

Every time you click "agree" online, you are sharing your data and authorizing companies to utilize it, to market and sell to you, profile you, and get to know you. This is why we need our digital twin, because it will work to protect our online identity and excel at conducting transactions on our behalf. Our digital twin will ensure that we can live in this new world without losing our shirt. Data is all-important, and it allows us to customize everything at will.

When we combine the concepts of Barrier-free Access, Democratized Egalitarianism, The Sharing Economy, and Transboundary Communities, we realize that we do not have to play within the traditional scope of roles or constructs anymore. We can be an enterprise of one competing at will and with equal value, and we can work to create our own virtual neighborhoods to deepen our connections and determine how we want to live and interact with others. These concepts will move us toward the new human renaissance, which we will talk more about in Chapter 11.

In the next few chapters, we are going to examine how this new digital economy will function, what role government and infrastructure will play, how we will meet this new social imperative, and what kind of regulatory and social frameworks will be required.

Some guidelines will be needed to help companies be more competitive as we move closer to Singularity.

CHAPTER NINE

THE DIGITAL BUSINESS IMPERATIVE

Whether you have signed up for a subscription service that sends you vitamins or tailored-to-fit clothes based on your preferences, you are now having a smart-enabled, automated relationship with the entities offering you products and services. As we said earlier in this book, things used to be very different: In the early twentieth century, if you wanted an automobile, Ford offered one model, the Model T, in one color, black. And people bought them by the millions. Today, buyers dictate what they want and the level of customization they need. They have flipped the supply and demand chains, and customized consumer demand is increasingly driving what companies produce and how they operate.

On our journey throughout this book, we have learned much about the customer demand–driven economy we find ourselves in, as well as the four pillars that will give rise to a new digital ecosystem. Hyperconvergence, Digital Moments, Augmented Reality, and Digital Twins are together providing a platform to experience the social components we saw in the last chapter that are changing the way we work and communicate. Democratized Egalitarianism, Barrier-free Access, The Sharing Economy, and Transboundary Communities will connect us to this new world.

So, how do we do not only do business in this new economy but thrive as we head toward Singularity? All of these new technologies and platforms for connecting represent a *digital imperative*, a vital obligation, for what we must do to reimagine our future and succeed. This imperative applies to both businesses and governments. The digital business imperative is forcing businesses to imagine how they will use the digital ecosystem in a manner that drives better value for the individual. The key word here is *imperative*—it is something that businesses *must* do to survive and grow. Similarly, the digital government imperative focuses on the need to balance appropriate regulation without stifling innovation.

The digital business imperative is a result of technology providing a framework for connecting with people in new ways.

To make sure we reach Singularity instead of obsolescence, we will need to invest in the Technology Prerequisites, learn how to interact with the technology pillars that are moving forward in development, and recalibrate how we are interacting with individuals to understand their personalized desires and needs. As we will see, there will be opportunities for business and a need for new controls for us to move forward safely.

Two Areas of Focus

To seize the opportunities inherent in Singularity, companies must focus on two tasks: 1) grow channels that maximize opportunities to market to individuals; and 2) make the right investments in digital infrastructure, commerce, and currency.

Individualized Demand

In the last chapter, we saw that technology is changing the way we work and communicate with each other. Increased access and a powerful voice are giving us direct access to the economy. This access comes at a low cost of entry, which enables many to earn money doing activities in nontraditional ways. And because we are connecting to the world differently, the digital business imperative requires us to reimagine how we will sell, buy, and interact, in a manner vastly different than in the Information Age. For businesses, that means being able to engage with their customers and buyers *directly*.

Directly is a word we are seeing a lot lately. In the old days, we would put up a billboard on a major freeway and hope that somebody driving by *indirectly* engaged with it. The direct, digital, interactive version of this is a restaurant that has analyzed your buying habits and patterns, figured out where you are every day at lunchtime, and sends texts to your phone encouraging you to come in for Taco Tuesday. Businesses will need to learn how to address people on a more one-to-one basis in this customer demand–driven economy.

Because the customer comes first in the digital economy, companies will need to personalize products, services, and solutions, and deliver them, made to order for the unique needs of individuals. Individuals are increasingly voicing what they want both intentionally and unintentionally— intentionally in that we are active "Yelpers," and advocates of our favorite brands and services on social media, and unintentionally in that we create a trail of data reflected in our "likes" on Facebook and how long we keep our TV remote hovered over *Friends* as we evaluate what we are going to watch tonight on Netflix. This data creates detailed consumer profiles that can be leveraged by the business collecting the data, or sold to other interested parties for market research. The more companies begin to understand their customers at an individual level, the more successful they will be at selling in this new economy.

Digital Infrastructure, Commerce, and Currency

For all this to work, we will need to have a high-quality network infrastructure, strong bandwidth availability, and the ability to connect. Businesses need to make investments in the Technology Prerequisites to build the digital infrastructure and ensure success in the new economy.

Since we live and work differently now than in the past, we will need to use and invest in platforms that accept cryptocurrency and digital payments. Our customers are demanding it more and more each day; the new business imperative demands it as well. In the near future, investing in a strategy around cryptocurrency to conduct transactions in a new digital economy will become the price of admission for business. That means digital capital investments in currencies like Bitcoin and its competitors Ethereum, Ripple, and others.

Advancements in cryptography and distributed computing over the last several years led to the arrival of blockchain, which serves as the backbone for validating and securing transactions. This technology has the potential to fundamentally change how business is conducted in a digitally connected world. Simply put, blockchain transactions are fast, *transboundary*, ubiquitous, difficult to fake, and decentralized. Traditional transactions have required confirmation and validation by a "trusted intermediary" such as a bank or an escrow firm.

But in the digital world, blockchain-based technologies can support this confirmation.

Still, the hype of cryptocurrencies is not likely to last. This is because the main reason for their interest is speculative. Also, cryptocurrencies cannot be manipulated by governments or the Federal Reserve, so the exchange rate and value are driven purely by the market. While the U.S. government has the ability to adjust interest rates and control the valuation of the dollar, nobody has the power to control the value of cryptocurrency. It is, so far, unregulated and untaxed. It is a free market, and it is continuously moving. Such currencies cannot go unregulated, as they can support black-market transactions and even illegal activity. But the bigger question becomes this: Will governments regulate cryptocurrencies and payment platforms? As we have discussed, this is unavoidable because governments cannot allow economic transactions to happen within their borders without some kind of taxation or regulation. As governments regulate these currencies, force transparency, and tax transactions, these currencies will lose favor. Ultimately, unlike government-backed currencies, there is no protection from losses or theft with cryptocurrency.

In the United States, for instance, your money is protected by the Federal Deposit Insurance Corporation, while cryptocurrencies have no such protection. As such, Bitcoin and others will not likely be the currencies of the future. That said, the underlying technology of blockchain will likely be used across many applications where transactions need to be validated, including banking, voting, social networks, identity networks, utilities, and healthcare.

As we advance toward Singularity, cryptocurrencies might initially prove popular and provide the foundation for global transactions. But participants execute transactions based on the trust and confirmation of peers, along with an agreed-upon set of rules, so it is likely that established currencies will win this race. And we will likely see established currencies like the U.S. dollar becoming more nimble and more digital. Today, mobile payment platforms like PayPal, Zelle, and Venmo can make digital transactions possible with most traditional currencies. These platforms will become part of the economic fabric in the years ahead because money movement is vital for microtransactions to occur. Therefore, it would be wise to stay a step ahead and invest in platforms that can accept digital currencies now and going forward. Businesses could stand to lose millions by not creating a pathway for their use.

Over- and Under-Regulating

The digital business imperative is a challenge for companies to connect in unique ways with their partners, customers, and stakeholders. How we do business in this new economy and ecosystem is going to depend on new rules and controls. Of course, the overregulation of new technologies can also suppress growth and innovation. Governments must enact balanced policies designed to ensure managed growth.

By way of example, in the late 1990s, the internet started becoming a popular way to communicate and conduct simple transactions. America Online, popularly known as AOL, promoted its service by sending discs in the mail, offering thousands of free online hours to prospective subscribers. It is ironic that these discs are now considered collectibles.[1] Any heavy regulation at this point could have killed the internet's potential. Instead, the U.S. government took a more prudent measure. The 1998 Internet Tax Freedom Act was passed by Congress and signed into law on October 21, 1998. At the time, President Bill Clinton and Vice President Al Gore supported the law because it was geared to avoid overregulating the fledgling internet. In fact, the objective of the legislation was to support the internet's use in commerce, education, and as a global communication tool. As the law was being formulated, specific discussions on Capitol Hill focused on how the sale of goods and services should be taxed on the internet—specifically,

---

1 Erin Blakemore, "Remember These Free AOL CDs? They're Collectibles Now!" *Smithsonian,* October 13, 2015, https://www.smithsonianmag.com/smart-news/aol-cd-rom-collecting-thing-180956902/.

how to get businesses operating online to pay sales tax, without impacting the growth of this new medium.

With regard to the issue of taxing online businesses, there has been a continuing debate about whether internet companies need to collect sales taxes if they do not have a brick-and-mortar location in the consumer's state. In 1992, the U.S. Supreme Court decided there was no need. Six years later, the Internet Tax Freedom Act prohibited state and local governments from taxing access or imposing discriminatory taxes on e-commerce.[2] Since then, some states have found a way around this and collect sales tax from online retailers.[3] For example, approximately forty-five states[4] now collect sales tax from purchases on Amazon, which has data centers and other facilities nationwide. And even if the retailer does not assess a tax, your state may still make you pay a tax on your purchase.[5] Many have argued that the recent surge in cybercurrencies is just another attempt to avoid taxable transactions.

---

2 Congressional Research Service, "The Internet Tax Freedom Act: In Brief," April 13, 2016, https://fas.org/sgp/crs/misc/R43772.pdf.

3 Don Reisinger, "Your State May Fight for Internet Sales Tax," *Fortune,* February 24, 2016, http://fortune.com/2016/02/24/state-internet-sales-tax/.

4 Amazon, "How Tax Is Calculated," https://www.amazon.com/gp/help/customer/display.html?nodeId=468512.

5 Darla Mercado, "10 More States Will Now Collect Sales Taxes from Amazon Shoppers," CNBC, February 1, 2017, https://www.cnbc.com/2017/02/01/10-more-states-will-now-collect-sales-taxes-from-amazon.html.

During the Clinton administration, the prevailing thought on the issue was this: *Let us punt on internet sales tax for now. Let the internet grow untethered.* Gore played a vital role in nurturing public use of the Web. As a congressman, he helped secure funding for the National Center for Super-computing Applications, where the Mosaic Web browser first was developed.[6]

There were efforts to regulate the internet in 1996, with the Communications Decency Act and the Child Pornography Prevention Act, both of which have been largely overturned.[7] Since then, broadband internet connections have not been regulated like basic telephone lines, and have remained fairly regulation-free. In 1998, FCC Chairman William Kennard said that internet services should not be classified as telecommunications. Doing so "could have significant consequences for the global development of the Internet," he said.[8]

---

6 Glen Kessler, "A Cautionary Tale for Politicians: Al Gore and the 'Invention' of the Internet," November 4, 2013, https://www.washingtonpost.com/news/fact-checker/wp/2013/11/04/a-cautionary-tale-for-politicians-al-gore-and-the-invention-of-the-internet/?utm_term=.15ef6fc25053.

7 National Coalition Against Censorship, "A Selective Timeline of the Internet and Censorship," http://ncac.org/resource/a-selective-timeline-of-the-internet-and-censorship.

8 Phil Kerpen, "Regulating Internet's Future by Changing the Past," *Forbes*, April 22, 2010, https://www.forbes.com/2010/04/22/broadband-fcc-regulation-opinions-contributors-phil-kerpen.html#22ebb7885d0a.

But there have been a number of successful efforts to regulate the Web. In the 1960s, 1970s, and 1980s, the federal government helped create today's internet by making competitive markets for modems and networking services, breaking telephone service monopolies up into separate units, and writing rules governing telephone and cable lines and companies.[9] In 2017, the Federal Communications Commission asked for public support to return to the light-touch regulatory framework that enabled an open internet to blossom over 20 years.[10]

Regulation is necessary, but it is a framework that is going to evolve over time. There is a perspective that government needs to regulate things *before* they emerge—but, as we have seen, this does not always happen. Because it has avoided taxes on transactions, the internet has thrived as an engine of growth and expression, and as the digital backbone of our economy. The Clinton administration encouraged commerce on the internet by not hindering it, and that allowed for innovation to happen continuously. It remains to be seen whether regulators will take a wait-and-see approach to forthcoming technologies.

---

9 Kevin Werbach, "Digital Tornado: The Internet and Telecommunications Policy," Federal Communications Commission working paper, March 1997, http://transition.fcc.gov/Bureaus/OPP/working_papers/oppwp29.pdf.
10 Federal Communications Commission, "Restoring Internet Freedom," https://www.fcc.gov/restoring-internet-freedom.

Regulation and Repercussions

For many of the new technologies, when and how regulation should happen has yet to be determined. The challenge we face in this new digital economy is building that regulatory framework. The digital revolution is likely to generate many unforeseeable transactions. Those will inevitably be followed by government entities proposing enlightened regulatory frameworks for many advancing technologies. This includes laws designed to protect individual privacy, safeguard data loss, enforce patents, regulate financial transactions, ensure product safety, and guard individual rights. There is a history of this, as governments have always lagged behind innovation. But the regulations eventually will materialize and help stabilize digital business models.

For example, when Elon Musk ultimately releases his fully autonomous Tesla self-driving car, he might utilize an e-commerce platform to connect to his supply chain so that we can buy, and he can deliver, that product directly. Imagine your new car driving itself directly to your home instead of it being manually delivered the way Teslas are today. And since the car will drive itself down the road, we will need an enlightened regulatory framework in case of accidents, malfunctions, and even deaths that could occur from its use. And, of course, Tesla is not the only automaker moving in this driverless direction: Ford CEO Jim Hackett said at the 2018 Consumer Electronics Show that the company is focusing not only on cars but on "transportation systems" based on building an open-source operating system for self-driving cars and industrial vehicles.[11] And GM is testing a ride-sharing fleet model, with autonomous, self-driving vehicles that will not have steering wheels or pedals.[12]

Additionally, some fairly thorny issues surround new technologies that test and/or access our DNA. Home DNA tester Ancestry.com is just one of many companies growing in popularity lately. For a small fee, Ancestry.com will analyze a swab of your saliva and return a detailed genetic analysis that includes an ethnic history. More than four million people have tried it.[13] But what are the regulatory implications? Who actually owns your DNA after it leaves your mouth? Does

---

11 Aaron Pressman and Adam Lashinsky, "Data Sheet—Ford CEO Says Cars Have Restricted Some Freedom," *Fortune,* January 10, 2018, http://fortune.com/2018/01/10/data-sheet-ford-ceo-jim-hackett-ces-2018/?utm_campaign=fortunemagazine&utm_source=twitter.com&utm_medium=social&xid=soc_socialflow_twitter_FORTUNE.
12 David Welch and Ryan Beene, "GM Drops the Steering Wheel and Gives Robot Driver Control," Bloomberg, January 12, 2018, https://www.bloomberg.com/news/articles/2018-01-12/gm-drops-the-steering-wheel-and-gives-the-robot-driver-control.
13 "Ancestry DNA Reaches 4 Million Customers in DNA Database" (blog), ancestry.com, April 27, 2017, https://blogs.ancestry.com/ancestry/2017/04/27/ancestrydna-reaches-4-million-customers-in-dna-database/.

anyone have a right to research it? Can you use this ethnic information on a census survey or to claim racial identity on a college application? What is your expectation of privacy?

Clients using many of these services appear to be granting a "perpetual, royalty-free, worldwide, transferable license" to use their DNA. In some cases, customers are also required to release the company from "all claims, liens, demands, actions or suits in connection with" their DNA.[14] That has led to concern among lawmakers. Senator Chuck Schumer of New York recently called for more scrutiny into DNA-testing company procedures, some of which he said put customers at risk for allowing their DNA to be sold to unknown third parties. He also called on the Federal Trade Commission to look into these companies' privacy policies.[15]

Another technology that uses our DNA, CRISPR, is raising additional concerns about regulation. CRISPR allows doctors, scientists, and researchers to target specific segments of genetic code to edit an individual's DNA. It allows them to use retroviruses to introduce DNA into a living cell within an organism and rewrite the DNA. With the right computer

14 "Ancestry Terms and Conditions," ancestry.com, https://www.ancestry.com/dna/en/legal/us/termsAndConditions.
15 Daniella Silva, "Senator Calls for More Scrutiny of Home DNA Test Industry," NBC News, November 26, 2017, https://www.nbcnews.com/news/us-news/senator-calls-more-scrutiny-home-dna-test-industry-n824031.

modeling and analytics, it could reasonably reengineer cells and eradicate any kind of genetic disease. The potential to solve chronic and genetic health issues is incredible.

So far, the U.S. Food and Drug Administration has approved CRISPR for cancer treatment clinical trials.[16] But editing and implanting animal and human embryos are still forbidden.[17] Broad application—and regulation—of the technology will involve "the participation of multiple constituencies in considering the most effective regulatory policies to address any potential risks," said the FDA's commissioner and senior policy adviser at the beginning of 2017.[18] In a perhaps alarmist assessment, a top U.S. intelligence official added gene editing, like CRISPR, to a list of threats posed by "weapons of mass destruction and proliferation."[19]

---

16 Emily Mullin, "FDA Approves Groundbreaking Gene Therapy for Cancer," *MIT Technology Review,* August 30, 2017, https://www.technologyreview.com/s/608771/the-fda-has-approved-the-first-gene-therapy-for-cancer/.

17 Megan Molteni, "Scientists Crispr the First Human Embryos in the U.S. (Maybe)," *Wired,* July 27, 2017, https://www.wired.com/story/scientists-crispr-the-first-human-embryos-in-the-us-maybe/.

18 Robert M. Califf and Ritu Nalubola, "FDA's Science-Based Approach to Genome Edited Products" (blog), U.S. Food & Drug Administration, January 18, 2017, https://blogs.fda.gov/fdavoice/index.php/tag/crispr/.

19 Antonio Regalado, "Top U.S. Intelligence Official Calls Gene Editing a WMD Threat," *MIT Technology Review,* February 9, 2016, https://www.technologyreview.com/s/600774/top-us-intelligence-official-calls-gene-editing-a-wmd-threat/.

New technologies, like the ones just described, affect the entire value chain. And the digital value chain is underpinning the digital business imperative, and as we will see, the social imperative and the human renaissance. It is not just buying goods and services—those are the easy examples. It is the right to protect our DNA, the molecule that carries our genetic instructions. It is about who we are, our relationship with our children, our peers—everything. We will have to find a socioeconomic model that works for most people. Cybercurrencies could be one of the ways to achieve that.

So, what is the right regulatory approach? What we are likely to see is that businesses willing to make investments based upon the synergy of the four technology pillars will develop the next advancements and innovations. But it will take time for governments to catch up. During this period, we are going to be in this "brave new world" as well as a new and hopeful period in history resulting from major changes in society. And, because of Democratized Egalitarianism, we now have a need for policies that protect free speech, but also protect those harmed by malicious social media that is factually incorrect or designed to cause damage.

Where We Are Headed

Regulations can be beneficial and protect society from new technologies that may be harmful without appropriate boundaries. Regulations provide us with the rules and confidence to invest and even take business risks. Of course, overregulation can have the negative impact of slowing innovation. In the United States, we have often swung between periods of over- and under-regulation.

As the digital ecosystem emerges, it is creating a new set of rules. It is constantly requiring new thinking and approaches to a world that is shifting so quickly. And as technologies continue to evolve, they require regulations to catch up just as fast, as people's buying habits and businesses change rapidly to adapt. The speed of this evolution, without adequate controls, is causing a number of thought leaders on the subject to express fear as we head toward Singularity.

In terms of the coming technological omnipresence, our view remains that there is a case for humanity. We will gain control of the technologies, and they will become part of our ecosystem to create better services for people. They will give us a stronger voice in our communities, allow us to communicate more effectively with our friends, have better social networks, and empower us to be more innovative. We will adapt quickly. As this technology races toward us so will our speed to deal with it. Governments are already reacting and will need to accelerate their efforts.

To survive in the digital economy, businesses must build continuous innovation into their DNA and governments simultaneously must become more flexible to allow for this to happen. The concept of the digital imperative means that both governments and businesses cannot avoid this change. Both will need to adapt to be relevant in the digital economy. If businesses are to prevail, they must adapt to the new digital ecosystem by identifying new customer touchpoints and models to generate revenue.

To start, businesses need to double down and make the appropriate investments in the Technology Prerequisites and in understanding the core elements of the digital economy. These prerequisites are the platform upon which businesses will communicate, sell, and innovate in the new economy. For governments, this means learning to engage citizens and constituents in a new manner, and with the four digital pillars in mind. Consider the opportunity to adopt new "e-government" platforms designed to aid businesses and people in the digital economy. Ultimately, new public-private partnerships will be born, and a balance will be achieved between ongoing innovation and the need for regulation.

CHAPTER TEN

THE SOCIAL IMPERATIVE

In 2006, when civil rights activist Tarana Burke coined the phrase "Me Too" to raise awareness about sexual abuse and assault, there was no way she could've known that eleven years later it would become a hashtag that would galvanize millions of women around the world to support each other and break the silence about sexual harassment and abuse in a variety of industries. Amid 2017's uncertainty and tumultuousness, in which the Women's March was launched and a number of technology, entertainment, and news industry executives were accused of harassment and assault, actress Alyssa Milano in a Twitter post asked survivors to reply with #MeToo. What happened next was unexpected: It rapidly turned into a viral movement in which many more allegations followed against

153

executives, comedians, actors, and politicians—and change soon started moving forward. In the first two weeks alone, close to 1.8 million people in eighty-five countries used the hashtag.[1]

Influenced by #MeToo, many people in the global film industry began working to launch new codes of conduct, attempting to change behaviors on and off set. The British film industry did so and members wore #NoPredators badges on sets; the Canadian film and TV industry said "MeToo" and offered up more robust, effective ways to report and prevent abuse; and the Swedish Film Institute introduced mandatory sexual conduct training for all companies applying for film subsidies.[2] Beyond the entertainment industry, many companies have started reevaluating their policies to create an environment where employees can feel safe. Harassment reports are expected to increase in 2018 as more victims feel empowered to raise their voices.[3]

---

1 Andrea Park, "#MeToo Reaches 85 Countries with 1.7M Tweets," CBS News, October 24, 2017, https://www.cbsnews.com/news/metoo-reaches-85-countries-with-1-7-million-tweets/.

2 Scott Roxborough, "How the #MeToo Movement Is Changing Showbiz Culture Worldwide," *Hollywood Reporter,* November 27, 2017, https://www.hollywoodreporter.com/news/how-metoo-movement-is-changing-showbiz-culture-worldwide-1061349.

3 Samantha Bomkamp, "#MeToo in 2018: Will the Movement Create Real Change in the Workplace?" *Chicago Tribune,* December 27, 2017, http://www.chicagotribune.com/business/ct-biz-metoo-sexual-harassment-future-20171214-story.html.

The movement also rippled across a number of ponds when, in early 2018, a professor of a top university in Beijing, China, was accused of sexually harassing a student, violating the school's code of conduct. While the student had publicly raised the issue of the professor's alleged harassment thirteen years prior, inspired by the #MeToo movement, her blog post about it exploded online and she encouraged others in China to come forward.[4]

What we have witnessed in the last few years is the magnifying power technology platforms provide to social movements. Technology can create a social imperative—a need to come forward as a result of one person or a small group of people challenging business and society to act differently—to change how we speak, operate, and even sell and offer products, services, and ideas.

Remember the viral "ice bucket challenge," in which people—celebrities, CEOs, everyone—dumped cold water on their heads to raise money for, and awareness of, ALS? It ended up raising $115 million to fund new research, all because

---

4 Philip Wen and Christian Shepherd, "Ripple Effect of #MeToo in China: Beijing Professor Dismissed Over Sexual Allegations," *Christian Science Monitor*, January 12, 2018, https://www.csmonitor.com/World/Asia-Pacific/2018/0112/ Ripple-effect-of-MeToo-in-China-Beijing-professor-dismissed-over-sexual-allegations.

people worked together for a cause that was completely driven by social media.[5]

The social imperative is all about the momentum created by social movements. This momentum is more powerful than ever as a result of the concepts of Barrier-free Access (limitless access to data and information) and Democratized Egalitarianism (our voice across social platforms). Thanks to our access to both unlimited information and global resources, a single voice now can be magnified to launch a social movement, drive fashion trends, or even impact elections. This social momentum must be considered by companies and organizations as we enter into the digital economy.

As such, the digital business imperative is not an option; it requires companies to build new digital value chains to connect them to data sources, revenue sources, stakeholders, and customers. The social imperative further augments the business imperative. Businesses should not use new technology platforms and digital value chains just as a new way to boost profits; the social imperative encourages businesses to align with social movements that speak to their customers. And just like the digital business imperative, companies must begin to

---

5 Katie Reilly, "Man Who Inspired Ice Bucket Challenge Dies at Age 46," *Time,* November 29, 2017, http://time.com/5042254/anthony-senerchia-ice-bucket-challenge-als/.

think of ways to connect with their customers on a sociological dimension. It is no longer a nice idea to have corporate social responsibility goals—it is essential for companies to be involved and "live" these goals through their social interactions.

In this new digital ecosystem, social movements create calls to action that thousands can take up in a matter of minutes. As providers of products and services, it will be essential to align ourselves with these movements in a way that speaks to our customers. Individuals directly tell us what they like and dislike, and businesses should respond appropriately with customized products and socially responsible solutions. When social media platforms enable and inform Transboundary Communities, Barrier-free Access, and The Sharing Economy, these platforms create social movements that penetrate the hearts, minds, and computer screens of millions at an unparalleled rate.

Communication Is Changing

How we communicate and work with each other is shifting. And unless we can shift along with it, we will not be able to have the kinds of social interactions that are possible in this new economy.

For example, have you called an airline's customer service line recently to air a problem? To reach an actual human being, first you have to jump through an automated system's hoops, voluminous menus, and options—only then to be put on interminable hold.

But increasingly, people are not choosing that option. Instead, they are going the self-help route, clicking over to the airline's website to instant message with a "chatbot," an AI platform built on a database of analytics and information about commonly asked questions. By 2020, average folks will have more conversations with bots than with customer service representatives. More than 85 percent of customer interactions will not require any human agent.[6]

We have even more effective routes than asking a bot for help. Let us say we are frequent travelers who make the same loop from Los Angeles to San Francisco and back, over and over again, for business. When we fly out in the morning, we notice that the same flight always lands hard, like an elbow to the chin, on the tarmac up north. What if we decided to skip the phone call and, instead, tweet about that airline's teeth-rattling landings? What if we decided to stream one of the landings on Facebook live and tag the airline? If others on that route liked the posts and continued to share or retweet them, they could become trending topics, perhaps even arouse

6 Christie Schneider, "10 Reasons Why AI-Powered, Automated Customer Service Is the Future," IBM, October 16, 2017, https://www.ibm.com/blogs/watson/2017/10/10-reasons-ai-powered-automated-customer-service-future/.

the attention of a local reporter. What if that one tweet got us an apology from the company's marketing division and a number of free upgrades to first class—and even went so far as changing how that airline trained its pilots to land their 737 aircraft in San Francisco? All of this activity would change how the airline operates, all based on a tweet. That is a simple, and certainly plausible, example of the clout of social platforms that allow for continuous feedback loops.

These social platforms will continue to shape the social imperative, including how we communicate with each other, personally and professionally, and what our expectations will be from businesses and other people. These platforms will also create different relationships among people, devices, and social groups.

What Consumers Say Goes

As we move forward, the question becomes, What opportunities will these new platforms bring for us to do business and work with each other? Well, the social imperative compels consumers to assert their feelings about a product, brand, or movement. These assertions can have tremendous impact on companies. Consumers can change how products are developed and manufactured—almost instantaneously.

Consider Elon Musk's recent decision to poll his customers by tweeting to ask what features they would like to see on the new Tesla. More than thirteen thousand sent in ideas for changes and new features, and Musk responded personally to a number of them, saying he would work on upgrades and new functionality for his vehicles. The speed at which we can experience new services and communicate with companies and others is allowing the social imperative to have a greater bearing on what companies do.

Keeping in mind the concept of Democratized Egalitarianism, technology platforms can empower anyone's voice and have the ability to change practices based on how consumers rate and share service and products online. As a recent survey of midsize and large businesses found, companies are more closely following what their customers are posting online: 42 percent of businesses are doing so to improve customer relationships, and 25 percent of them are "listening" in an effort to improve products.[7] In the coming years, as technology advances continue to grow individuals' digital footprint, the number of companies actively monitoring what their customers say online will increase.

In an effort to remain competitive and responsive, GM has formed a special global unit dedicated to its more than

---

7 Jess Shankleman, Electric Car Sales Are Surging, IEA Reports," Bloomberg, June 7, 2017, https://www.bloomberg.com/news/articles/2017-06-07/electric-car-market-goes-zero-to-2-million-in-five-years.

150 social media channels to pay special attention and listen to customers' concerns and issues. The unit, established to enhance the customer experience and resolve issues in real time, handles more than six thousand monthly interactions with customers. Some of the information in online user forums is sent to GM's quality and engineering teams to aid in product development.

In one instance, team members found a blog in which a customer was having an issue with a car's climate-control system. After the blog attracted comments and thousands of views, GM took action. Working with engineering, it identified the problem and then sent a service message to dealers explaining how to fix the module. And the customer had not yet even asked GM for help.[8]

Social platforms also provide companies with new methods to drive economic behavior. Ultimately, with that power, people will be able to effect massive changes in businesses overnight. Businesses are obliged to be more flexible to address fluid, almost-instant demand requirements. And if you are a company, you must start paying attention to, and investing in, new platforms for connection.

---

8 Alicia Boler-Davis, "How GM Uses Social Media to Improve Cars and Customer Service," *Harvard Business Review,* February 12, 2016, https://hbr. org/2016/02/how-gm-uses-social-media-to-improve-cars-and-customer-service.

The Social Agenda and Demand Creation

Consumers are more likely than ever to buy based upon their social agenda, and companies are taking it seriously.

Imagine we are a large auto manufacturer that is planning for the future. If we have not by now, we are starting to realize that having all of our eggs in one basket will not satisfy our customers or allow us to remain competitive. For the first century of the automobile, consumers demand defaulted to internal combustion engines—the most effective automobile technology at the time. But as we race toward Singularity, if we are still only placing our bets on diesel and gasoline engines, and not investing in new technologies, we will be falling further and further behind.

Luckily, for us, and for many other car companies, electric cars are making the jump from expensive niche products to practical modes of transportation due to superior performance, viable price points, and the environmental interests of customers. More carmakers are releasing or planning to release electric vehicles for their buyers, a trend that is only growing over time.[9] In fact, last year, plug-in and battery-powered vehicles on roads

9 "Are Consumers Ready to Hit the Gas on Electric Cars?" PBS podcast, July 19, 2017, https://www.pbs.org/newshour/show/consumers-ready-hit-gas-electric-cars.

worldwide rose 60 percent from the year before, despite being a nonexistent category five years earlier.[10] Worldwide electric car ownership is expected to hover between forty million and seventy million by 2025, a threefold increase from forecasts for 2020.[11]

In this example, social values and environmental interests are driving customers to want new products. They will likely drop companies, and their products, in a minute, if those companies do not seem to be connected to their social agenda. What are traditional auto manufacturers to do? The social imperative has quickly shifted demand for their products. And it is not just a little shift—it is a new paradigm.

In another example, Tyson Foods, the biggest poultry producer in the U.S., announced it would eliminate the use of human antibiotics on chickens by mid-2017 due to the loud voices of customers, health experts, and consumer advocacy groups. The food supplier said it was responding to consumer demand.[12]

10 Jess Shankleman, Electric Car Sales Are Surging, IEA Reports," Bloomberg, June 7, 2017, https://www.bloomberg.com/news/articles/2017-06-07/electric-car-market-goes-zero-to-2-million-in-five-years.
11 International Energy Agency, "Global EV Outlook 2017," https://www.iea.org/publications/freepublications/publication/GlobalEVOutlook2017.pdf.
12 Jacob Bunge, "Tyson Joins the Flock on Curbing Antibiotics," *Wall Street Journal,* April 28, 2015, https://www.wsj.com/articles/tyson-joins-the-flock-on-curbing-antibiotics-1430208002.

Companies like Tyson will pay more attention to social movements as the "time to market" window shrinks and products and services need to meet this instant demand. The social imperative is perfecting the demand curve, helping companies figure out what consumers want and then giving them exactly that.

When we talk about the social imperative, the power of communication to activate and mobilize demand is truly amazing. The social imperative drives immediate demand for something, whether it is an underserved political group or a product, or information, news, and services. Technologies give microcommunities a voice and the ability to communicate their unique opinions and views in a manner that they never could before.

The social imperative is all about what society can do on these new digital platforms, communicating with each other to drive demand for new products, services, and information. Businesses of today and tomorrow will need to become scientists of the social imperative, because someone is going to have to take advantage of all this information.

In the next chapter, we will see that the digital economy, powered by these social platforms, will provide an opportunity for a human renaissance, with the digital imperative and social imperative as building blocks.

The new human renaissance will unleash infinite opportunities for humanity. As we reach Singularity, we are going to have enhanced automation, less human labor, as well as a deep and specialized understanding of our customers. All of those things will create more value and possibility for people. In the future, this means people will have more time to create opportunities and innovate.

CHAPTER ELEVEN

THE NEW HUMAN RENAISSANCE

Singularity, as we have discussed, will spawn a new human renaissance. And, contrary to popular belief and rhetoric, it will not be the end of humankind. The idea that "[i]n the end the machines will win"[1] presupposes that AI is a competitor to humankind. This in itself is a huge leap. It suggests that we are in some type of race for survival against an insidious AI species that is destined to usurp human existence with its malevolence and desire to destroy us. Certainly, this cannot be true.

There is no denying that AI needs to be regulated. But that is true mostly because of the potential for misuse of

---

1 Elon Musk, tweet, August 11, 2017, https://twitter.com/elonmusk/status /896166762361704450?lang=en.

this technology by its human masters. AI is neither sentient nor living. AI has no feelings and it is not competing with humanity, because it is simply a tool programmed by humans. History has taught us that humanity has always been wary of innovation. We have always feared machines, as they can outperform humans. AI is no different, and our distrust of it is no less. That said, if one understands the ages of human development, technological innovation is not something to fear. AI is no different than prior human creations. And, while it promises to automate many human activities, it is far from replacing human beings altogether.

The progress of artificial intelligence is a significant topic for us to consider as we move forward toward Singularity, but we realize it is not everyone's top worry. In a recent survey, fifty Nobel Prize winners ranked AI eighth on the list of the biggest threats to humankind, behind environmental degradation, nuclear war, drug resistance, and a few others.[2] Furthermore, as we have expressed in this book, we subscribe to a more hopeful view that the onset of Singularity will create a new human renaissance that will be a time of great opportunity—a positive, empowering case for humanity. This era will give us

2 Jack Grove, "Do Great Minds Think Alike? The THE/Lindau Nobel Laureates Survey," Times Higher Education, August 31, 2017, https://www. timeshighereducation.com/features/do-great-minds-think-alike-the-the-lindau-nobel-laureates-survey#survey-answer.

more time for self-actualization and meaningful relationships with people around us.

However, we recognize that the hysteria being drummed up in media and tech circles is growing and can feel quite real. In late 2017, there was even a movie called *Singularity*, starring John Cusack, in which a line of AI-aided supercomputers emerges that is designed to end all wars—but the computers soon determine humans are the main cause of violence, and they work to destroy humanity.

The biggest worry for some is whether future technology will benefit or hurt us. In the opening chapters, we looked at how our relationship with technology has constantly changed through the ages. Each wave of advancement has caused anxiety or paranoia that the new technology would damage ourselves, society, and our world.

For example, the telephone was seen as an invasion of privacy that could give off electric shocks and be a conduit for evil spirits. In 1890, Mark Twain wrote a Christmas card spreading good wishes to everyone except the inventor of the telephone.[3] Some feared it carried disembodied voices and

---

3 Aaron Smith, "Record Share of Americans Now Own Smartphones, Have Home Broadband," Pew Research Center, January 12, 2017, http://www.pewresearch.org/fact-tank/2017/01/12/evolution-of-technology/.

would lead to the end of people meeting face to face.[4] Some took a dim view of cassette recorders as devices that would destroy the music industry because people would tape records at home. "Computerphobia" took hold in the early 1980s, when the home computer was first being introduced.[5]

Technological changes create an air of distress only until we stop fighting, lower our fears, adapt, and move on. And Singularity will be just another period of accelerating innovation (albeit more rapid than other periods). We believe that advances in AI and other technologies will make us more free. It will be the start of a human renaissance.

Building the case for humanity means having faith that we are all not going to turn into cyborgs—due to some synthesis of humans and machines—that Terminators are not going to take over the world, and that artificial intelligence will not extinguish us. The new human renaissance will be the end result of all of the technologies—the existing, emerging, and future pillars and rules we have been discussing. It is the answer to the question "what will Singularity be like?" In essence, it

---

4 Natasha Lomas, "Humanity Has Always Feared Technology. In the 21st Century, Are We Right to Be Afraid?" zdnet.com, November 25, 2011, http://www.zdnet.com/article/humanity-has-always-feared-technology-in-the-21st-century-are-we-right-to-be-afraid/.
5 Clinton Nguyen, "7 World-Changing Inventions That Were Ridiculed When They Came Out," Business Insider, August 2, 2016, http://www.businessinsider.com/inventions-that-were-ridiculed-2016-8?r=UK&IR=T.

will be a world full of time and opportunities for us to solve the grand challenges and innovate in ways we never would have thought possible.

We Are Short on Time

In the modern economy of the last thirty years, we have lost something we have had in abundance for thousands of years: time. If we look at it in terms of the last thousand years, we could argue that, historically, human beings have had more time than we do today. Now, we are frantically rushing from task to task.

Today, we are engineered to continuously run, run, run. We are constantly consulting our phones, and our relationship with technology is all-encompassing—the world's information is automatically at our fingertips. We have grown accustomed to having less and less time, packing our days and calendars, every minute, every second.

It makes sense as more and more of us remain glued to our phones for both our social and professional needs: 77 percent of Americans own a smartphone, a number that has more than doubled since 2011.[6] And we are getting more connected worldwide: 50 percent of the global population of 7.5 billion uses the internet, and 34 percent are active mobile

---

6 Aaron Smith, "Record Share of Americans Now Own Smartphones, Have Home Broadband," Pew Research Center, January 12, 2017, http://www. pewresearch.org/fact-tank/2017/01/12/evolution-of-technology/.

social media users. In the U.S., the numbers are higher: 71 percent use the internet and 53 percent actively use social media phone apps.[7] Millennials alone spent more than 223 minutes a day on the mobile internet last year—more than double the amount compared to 2012.[8] Overall, U.S. users spent more than two and a half hours per day on mobile devices by the end of 2016, nearly doubling the time from 2012.[9]

All of this time on our phones is leading to a big problem: we are more stressed out than ever. In a recent survey, more than 60 percent of U.S. workers said they were stressed at least three days per week—nearly half said they worked nonrequired weekends, and more than half worked overtime. About 56 percent wanted to reduce stress to improve their quality of life, and a majority said they would rather be spending more time with their children.[10]

---

7 Simon Kemp, "Digital in 2017: Global Overview," wearesocial.com, January 24, 2017, https://wearesocial.com/special-reports/digital-in-2017-global-overview.

8 Statista, "Daily Time Spent on Mobile by Millennial Internet Users Worldwide from 2012 to 2017 (in Minutes)," https://www.statista.com/statistics/283138/millennials-daily-mobile-usage/.

9 Jeff Dunn, "'Smartphone Addiction' Seems to Only Be Getting Stronger," Business Insider, May 25, 2017, http://www.businessinsider.com/people-spending-more-time-on-smartphones-chart-2017-5.

10 Paychex, "Workplace Stress Is on the Rise," March 1, 2017, https://www.paychex.com/articles/human-resources/work-more-stress-less.

Researchers in France were so concerned about how we cannot seem to unplug that its government introduced legislation last year giving workers "the right to disconnect" to counteract the always-on work culture that can lead to exhaustion and burnout.[11]

Much of the reason people are so busy today is that we live in a culture that revolves around some type of capital and capital demand. We *have* to make money, then more and more. We are always moving; we cannot rest. But are we going too far? We have become a hyperfast society, where very little is going on that we are having *thoughtful* dialogue about—we are just reacting. We are hardly reflecting, pondering, or even preparing. The art of thinking and contemplation may not necessarily be lost, but it sure feels like it is not being developed now.

Solving the Grand Challenges

The good news for us is that the pillars of the digital economy are maturing. Hyperconvergence, Digital Moments, Augmented Reality, and Digital Twins—the building blocks that define what it is to live in the realm of Digital Singularity—are all nearly here and are giving rise to new platforms for communication and interaction. In turn, these platforms

11 Katie Beck, "France's Battle Against an "Always-On" Work Culture," BBC, May 8, 2017, http://www.bbc.com/capital/story/20170507-frances-battle-against-always-on-work-culture.

have streamlined access to goods, services, and information in a very customized way.

We will depend more heavily on the next generation of technology, but it will be less intrusive in our day-to-day lives. It will continue to enhance and simplify our lives but will function every second in the background. We are not there yet, but devices are getting smaller and less physically invasive. We are moving from symbiosis to technological omnipresence, where our surrounding technology will be acting on our behalf, with little to no effort on our end. Our TV will allow us to one-click-purchase our favorite soccer shoes instantly as we watch. Our digital twin will pay our bills, schedule grocery shipments, invest on our behalf, and more. Our work environments will be optimized with AI scheduling meetings and answering emails for us. Our current, active role with technology will drastically decrease as the four pillars mature. These advances will eventually take on a large decision-making role in many mundane activities that consume our lives on a daily basis. Singularity will usher in a new human renaissance focused on gaining back lost time—not time to focus on how we can become more productive, but to spend solving some of the greatest, most pervasive challenges of humankind.

As we have more time, what are we going to do with ourselves? We will turn back the course of a thousand years to what is more normal for humanity, a more balanced scorecard as it pertains to how we spend our time. We will begin to observe, communicate, and reflect again, and we will tackle, head on, the basic, fundamental problems that have been plaguing humanity for hundreds of years.

By 2030, the world population is predicted to grow to 8.3 billion people, from 6.9 billion just twenty years earlier,[12] and that puts pressure on developing countries throughout the world to ensure they have enough water for everything from agriculture and industry to basic hygiene and health. The growing population is already stressing supplies of food, water, and utilities.

Currently, the world is not on the right path to end world hunger by 2030, especially in Africa, India, and parts of Central America, according to a recent Brookings Institute report.[13] There are many reasons, from violent conflicts and weather disasters to climate change, extreme rural poverty,

12 United Nations, "Water and Food Security," October 23, 2010, http://www.un.org/waterforlifedecade/food_security.shtml.
13 Geoffrey Gertz, Homi Kharas, John McArthur, and Lorenz Noe, "When Will Things Change? Looking for Signs of Progress on Ending Rural Hunger," Brookings Institution, October 14, 2017, https://www.brookings.edu/research/when-will-things-change-looking-for-signs-of-progress-on-ending-rural-hunger/?utm_campaign=Brookings%20Brief&utm_source=hs_email&utm_medium=email&utm_content=57356746.

and inaction by unfocused policymakers. In 2016, the United Nations announced that the number of chronically malnourished rose for the first time in years, to 815 million.[14] About 844 million people lack drinking water, and globally, nearly two billion people use contaminated water, the World Health Organization found.[15]

Despite this disturbing news, Digital Singularity provides hope that humanity will have more time to focus on grand challenges such as solving world hunger. With the disruption of legacy jobs, as in prior ages, we will have more time to redirect our energies toward new challenges and innovations. Many of these innovations will focus on cleaning the environment, solving global poverty, and improving education. We predict that by 2030, 100 percent of people in developing countries will have access to food, compared to 87.1 percent now,[16] and 100 percent will have access to clean and affordable water, up from 91 percent at present.[17] And by 2030, we predict there will be universal access to utilities, up from 80 percent

14 FAO, IFAD, UNICEF, WFP, and WHO, "The State of Food Security and Nutrition in the World 2017," http://www.fao.org/3/a-I7695e.pdf.
15 World Health Organization, "Drinking-water" (fact sheet), July 2017, http://www.who.int/mediacentre/factsheets/fs391/en/.
16 United Nations, "17 Goals to Transform Our World: Goal 2," http://www.un.org/sustainabledevelopment/hunger/.
17 United Nations, "17 Goals to Transform Our World: Goal 6," http://www.un.org/sustainabledevelopment/water-and-sanitation/.

now.[18] There will also be more money spent, globally, on life sciences research and development, to the tune of more than $200 billion—a big leap from just under $100 billion twenty years ago. All of this will then lead to longer lives, pushing global life expectancy to seventy-seven years by 2045, up from just seventy-one now.[19]

Think of it this way: If you have power, you have everything. You can make potable water—you can desalinate the earth's oceans—and you can put the planet on a more sustainable path. If you have power, you can keep people warm, grow food, and even create industry and strengthen and increase the economy. As we achieve food, water, and power independence, we will have plentiful time as human beings to solve even more of the grand challenges.

One of the biggest issues facing us today is solving the global carbon emissions problem. In Al Gore's *An Inconvenient Sequel: Truth to Power* documentary, he observes that the technology being developed today is giving us an opportunity to reverse some frightening environmental trends. If we could reduce

---

18 United Nations, "17 Goals to Transform Our World: Goal 7," http://www.un.org/sustainabledevelopment/energy/.

19 United Nations, "Global Life Expectancy," June 21, 2017, https://www.un.org/development/desa/publications/graphic/wpp2017-global-life-expectancy.

pollution and move to clean energy, we could have unlimited energy and water. We could actually *green* Africa and the Middle East. But it will take a large shift in perspective: "The next generation would be justified in looking back at us and asking, 'What were you thinking? Couldn't you hear what the scientists were saying? Couldn't you hear what Mother Nature was screaming at you?' This movement is in the tradition of every great movement that has advanced humankind," Gore says in the documentary. Due to new technology, we are slowly taking our first, preliminary steps toward ending the destructive effect of carbon emissions on our environment.

You might be asking yourself, "Can we really take on the world's grand challenges?" Look no further than the Human Genome Project. The mapping of the human genome seemed like a monumental, incredible task just sixty-five years ago, when little was known about the genetic factors that cause disease. In 1953, Francis Crick and James Watson first described the structure of DNA[20]—and in 2003, the sequencing of the entire human genome's three billion base pairs of DNA was first completed.[21]

---

20 National Institutes of Health, "Human Genome Project," https://report.nih.gov/NIHfactsheets/ViewFactSheet.aspx?csid=45.
21 National Human Genome Research Institute, "An Overview of the Human Genome Project," https://www.genome.gov/12011238/an-overview-of-the-human-genome-project/.

The work of the Human Genome Project, a collaboration between governmental and scientific organizations around the world, has now helped identify more than 1,800 disease genes. And we believe this process will only keep progressing. Billions of human genomes will be sequenced and digitized by 2030, up from tens of millions of genomes now. If we can use innovation to unite in mapping our own astoundingly complex DNA, our emerging technology resources and social platforms will provide the means to collaboratively tackle large, complicated issues as we move into Singularity.

Higher-Order Pursuits

In this new human renaissance, since we will have drastically improved the ways in which we can provide for the basic needs of all mankind, we will have time to explore the very essence of meaning in our lives. In his hierarchy of needs theory, Maslow proposed that as basic needs are met, a person may focus on higher-order endeavors. Having sufficient food, water, and power will allow us to rise above the first two stages of Maslow's pyramid, physiological needs and safety needs. We will then be working on belongingness needs and esteem needs as we reach the pinnacle of the pyramid, self-actualization, or achieving our full potential as humans.

Since we will have access to limitless tools and data, as well as to healthcare, power, food, water, and shelter, we will be able to focus on self-actualization and having more meaning in our lives. We will truly focus on higher-order pursuits.

After solving the grand challenges, we will have time to be together, philosophize, socialize, write, and think. We will have time to dream and to create, and we will advance intellectually. What we will find is a sustained period of human innovation, which will be possible because more of humanity will be freed from worrying about basic needs. We will be able to generate more insights, ideas, and innovations to accomplish feats like traveling to Mars or solving the next far-reaching challenges. We will be able to create more value for humanity.

With abundant resources and time, we will have access to unrestrained opportunity to be an "enterprise of one" and create our own possibilities to make a living. Businesses will be compelled to structure their work environments in a way that will allow their employees to develop these humanity-changing ideas as well.

Providing for All

One of the worries that some in the technology sector have expressed is that, as we move into Singularity, there will be more automation, and fewer traditional jobs. Futurist Ray Kurzweil believes that Singularity will bring some bad but much good, especially with respect to jobs—the problem, he says, is we have not invented them yet.[22] We agree, because these jobs are likely in industries that do not exist, although we are getting a taste of what is to come as we evaluate the many developing technologies and their potential applications.

We cannot fully detail exactly what the opportunities will be, but we know there will be fewer traditional jobs. The jobs of the future will be driven by emerging digital ecosystems. For example, we can expect new opportunities to be driven by the Technology Prerequisites. This means that jobs will emerge via blockchain, IOT, analytics, automation, and cybersecurity. We will also see specialization emerge that supports the social imperative. Imagine going to a therapist to discuss your distress that your "followers" are dropping, or engaging a lawyer to recover damages from an online libel claim.

The case for humanity is strong and there will be jobs, but it will take time. In the near term, we will see job losses, but the incredible leaps and bounds in innovation will create new categories of jobs and businesses. The forthcoming innovation will transform jobs and how people work. In the age of Singularity, there will be fewer "traditional" jobs, positions that were previously 9 a.m. to 5 p.m. each day, in which the company took

---

22 Michal Lev-Ram, "Why Futurist Ray Kurzweil Isn't Worried About Technology Stealing Your Job," *Fortune*, September 24, 2017, http://fortune.com/2017/09/24/futurist-ray-kurzweil-job-automation-loss/.

care of you for much of your professional life. Through 2030, automation will greatly affect the global workforce. Somewhere between four hundred million and eight hundred million jobs could be eliminated or displaced due to automation. Around 50 percent of work activities will be automated, and about 9 percent of 2030 labor demand will be in new occupations that do not yet exist.[23] For many, the economic model will likely revolve around enterprise-of-one opportunities: contract writers and coders, for-hire executives, and in-the-moment professionals in a variety of industries and verticals.

The bigger question then becomes, what are people going to do if robots displace millions of workers, especially in lower-skilled positions, and new industries and opportunities are not yet fully developed? We will need to figure out how to support these workers, and that may mean moving toward more of a social contract. The idea is not exactly new: American revolutionary Thomas Paine believed the government should offer economic support to its vulnerable citizens, and suggested the idea in 1796.[24]

23 James Manyika, Susan Lund, Michael Chui, Jacques Bughin, Jonathan Woetzel, Parul Batra, Ryan Ko, and Saurabh Sanghvi, "What the Future of Work Will Mean for Jobs, Skills, and Wages," McKinsey & Company, November 2017, https://www.mckinsey.com/global-themes/future-of-organizations-and-work/what-the-future-of-work-will-mean-for-jobs-skills-and-wages.
24 Thomas Paine National Historical Association, "Paine on Basic Income and Human Rights," http://thomaspaine.org/paine-on-basic-income-and-human-rights.html.

The concept is starting to take shape now, especially in Silicon Valley's tech corridors. Facebook cofounder and CEO Mark Zuckerberg and Y Combinator president Sam Altman have been pushing forward the idea as a way to combat automation's effect on the global workforce.[25] And the area's U.S. Representative Ro Khanna recently unveiled a bill calling for a $1.4 trillion expansion of the Earned Income Tax Credit to create a basic income, via tax credits, for the bottom 20 percent of wage earners.[26]

These discussions about basic income and universal healthcare are happening because we recognize that there is some minimal human standard. We realize there may not be gainful employment for everyone, at least for now, while we are on our way to Singularity. We are starting to think about how to help others now.

So, let us move forward and not be afraid. The new human renaissance will offer infinite opportunity, information, and

25 Issie Lapowsky, "Money: The Surprising Effects of a Basic Income Supplied by Government," *Wired*, November 12, 2017, https://www.wired.com/story/free-money-the-surprising-effects-of-a-basic-income-supplied-by-government/?mbid=nl_111317_daily_list1_p2.

26 "Sen. Sherrod Brown and Rep. Ro Khanna Introduce Landmark Legislation to Raise the Wages of Working Families," press release, September 13, 2017, https://khanna.house.gov/media/press-releases/release-sen-sherrod-brown-and-rep-ro-khanna-introduce-landmark-legislation.

access to help everyone achieve happiness. But happiness, alone, is not going to be measured by financial success. It will be determined by building stronger relationships, and by innovating, being creative, and restoring balance in our lives.

There is an opportunity to jump off the treadmill, to get out of the rat race. Digital Singularity will not just give us health, opportunity, and information—it will connect us to each other, in more meaningful ways than we have ever experienced in humanity.

CHAPTER TWELVE

THE POWER OF THE INDIVIDUAL

Throughout this book, we have defined a number of technological and economic terms. We referred to these as both prerequisites and pillars for the digital economy. We have been building the hopeful, opportunity-driven case for humanity amid some prominent but alarmist views of Digital Singularity.

When we talk about the case for humanity, we are focused on how Digital Singularity frees us from the pains of the Information Age. Our calendars, email, meetings, and mobile phones dominate our time. Digital Singularity promises to take these processes off our plate, automate them, and give us more time to tackle issues that are most significant to humanity as a whole. On our way, we have begun to understand the new technologies coming into play and how they are changing the relationships of customers and individuals. At this point, a final question remains: How should business adapt to the changing economic conditions associated with Digital Singularity? In other words, how does all of this change our businesses, and what must companies, individuals, and governments do to prepare as we head into the future?

The answer is simpler than you might think. Due to our customer demand–driven economy, all of our increased social connections and transactions are designed for industry and the world to sell to and empower the individual—the "economy of one." This is something businesses need to be aware of, focus on, and pursue as we head toward Singularity.

New Models Are Emerging

Hyperloop technology, one of Elon Musk's many visionary projects, provides an interesting example of where we believe business is headed. Today, there are a number of competitive companies investing in the Hyperloop system, with the goal of creating a nearly frictionless tube designed to move a pod at high speed, carrying both humans and cargo. One of these companies is Hyperloop Transportation Technologies. What makes this company unique is how it is operating, investing, and growing in the new shared economy.

In the traditional business model, a large company lists a job, you apply for it, and if you are hired, you receive a salary and benefits package that varies depending on the position and industry. As we have discussed, the gig economy that is the backbone of the economy of one functions much differently. Hyperloop Transportation Technologies, an example of the emerging nontraditional employment model, works along these lines: Instead of just creating another big corporation centered on a technology, the founders decided to seek out the best and brightest with expertise in different areas and attract them with shared ownership for their work. People can put in as little as ten hours per week, working on their own time. Their reward: earning equity in the form of stock options. So far, more than eight hundred people have signed on as collaborators, and the project is surging ahead, gathering data and solving problems to bring the Hyperloop to reality.

Hyperloop Transportation Technologies also brings up a second point about the new economy we are facing now. Since people are "paid" for their works in different ways, this affects the funding and financing of businesses. Companies have usually been funded through private equity venture capital or a variety of investment banking options. Today, because of this nontraditional employment model, the investment can take the form of the "sweat labor" of individuals who possess specific proficiencies and knowledge. Think of it as a type of grassroots funding for companies and startups. This is a new economic reality, something we all need to take note of as we do business.

We have seen other examples of companies operating in this new sharing economy, where workers with diverse strengths divvy up profits, payments, or ownership, all while collaborating on a project and having the freedom to commit whatever time they have available. The online design provider 99designs is just one of many. These companies provide a platform that allows anyone, even people who are employed and potentially competing for that same work, to be part of it. But beware: Workers moonlighting in various capacities will ultimately begin to chip away market share from these same companies. The gig economy that powers individuals is only growing larger—as are the ranks of independent workers—as people find unconventional ways to learn, earn, and reinvent themselves.

This nontraditional employment model is something that more established companies will need to address. They will also have to figure out how they can take advantage of it. Will they need to worry about whether their own employees might undermine or erode a project they are bidding for, maybe even compete against them—through a Transboundary Community, as part of The Sharing Economy—for that same work?

Perhaps, as that is a challenge we are beginning to see due to the level of anonymity that exists in the market today.

How Did We Get Here?

Not too long ago, depending on the industry, we sold to hundreds of millions of people using mass production, a global supply chain, and a retail business model for product distribution. Today, we are still reaching out to millions upon millions, but *how* we do so has changed. Our products and services are more customized to individuals' needs, as we are now able to identify and recognize their desires and preferences through analytics. As such, our relationships and interactions with a product better support individuals' requirements. Consider your online purchases of a tailored shirt, shoes, or any other kind of product or service.

Years ago, we would segment the U.S. economy into categories—say, affluent, middle, and low income—and then we would work to find a model to address each one of the demographic and socioeconomic groups. Now, it is a much more specific process. With the technology pillars and Digital Singularity, we do not need to address whole groups of people. We can address them individually.

If we take a look at the traditional value chain versus a digital value chain, we are learning to put the individual first instead of concentrating solely on the manufacturing efforts. Between changes in the way we communicate and the impact of technology on the underlying social fabric, we have an opportunity to engage our clients, customers, employees, and families in a different way.

In previous ages, things were very different. Governments had power, business was controlled, and the common man did not have the direct ability to talk to anyone at the top of the business food chain. But the landscape has shifted.

Now, individuals have Barrier-free Access to the global stage, a bigger voice with Democratized Egalitarianism, and connections to multiple ecosystems of people through Transboundary Communities. They can operate globally and have the opportunity to participate in the shared economy. Today, it takes just one person to bring down a company as a whistleblower, start a social movement, like #MeToo, or compete on equal terms against a megacorporation. This same person can give critical feedback and get a call from the CEO of a major airline by alerting the company to a problem via a social platform. In the new digital economy, the power of one person is incredible, and how businesses and governments respond to this power will define the new digital economy.

When we talk about Democratized Egalitarianism, what is that, really? The power of individuals to tweet about the president, make a comment or a review, share when they like something, and assert strongly when they do not. In this new economy, everyone has a voice, and as we approach Singularity, our focus is changing from the indefinite to the individual. We are moving from an economy designed to support groups of people to one that will be geared toward a single person.

Starting now, the economy of one is everything. It is where all of our new platforms for interaction and building deep relationships are leading us. It is giving people tremendous power, time, and value. It is the ability for organizations to tailor products and services for each person, regardless of socioeconomic status, geography, or education level. This customization is all based on the person's specific preferences, wants, and needs, which we are learning more about with every interaction and transaction. We can interact with these stakeholders in a manner that is richer and more immersed in technology, but is, in many ways, more human and personal.

What Businesses Must Do

Digital Singularity is the fundamental understanding that a single individual can drive economic change, compete on the global stage, trigger social movements, and influence demand patterns and trends. As such, businesses must be prepared to develop new employment models, as well as new ways to protect intellectual property, socially market to people through Transboundary Communities, and collaboratively innovate through the shared economy.

Whatever industry you are in, it is critical to connect with people differently by investing in digital value chains and technologies that provide transactional automation. This automation, in the form of a digital moment, will not only provide better analytics and intelligence, it will also free humanity from mundane and repetitive tasks. Imagine a world where your email, groceries, shopping, household chores, and financial management are all automated. To build these new value chains, we must embrace the Four Pillars of Digital Singularity as the foundation for this automation.

The social enterprise will drive a large percentage of business transactions and give power to people. Even with this great digital value chain, nothing will happen without the social enterprise. *Social* today means our interactions on platforms like Facebook, Twitter, Instagram, and Snapchat. Soon enough, that social aspect will become the thread connecting everything we do and are. And technology will be very supportive of our social relationships and day-to-day life, without giving us an ounce of interference. It will be omnipresent, yet simply disappear into the background.

That is why industries will need to know who we are, not just physically but socially, online: not only what we like to read, the clothes we wear, and what we like to buy—but what we believe. Without understanding the social enterprise, businesses will operate with an outdated view of the world and the analog value chain that has persisted for decades. The social enterprise tells us so much more about who people are and what they want and like—and that data is being sold today.

Creating the digital value chain and understanding the social enterprise are going to require investments in new technologies to rebuild the industry and transform companies. It might be a tough transition for some. For example, will a large auto manufacturer be prepared to operate this way? Will it be able to understand digital value chains and how to automate them? Will it leverage the social enterprise to move past standard ways of building and selling cars? How does a business evolve from one way of selling—cars, washing machines, various services—to a new, focused way of targeting and interacting? All industries can get there by shifting investments in outmoded technologies and business processes into adopting and developing technologies of tomorrow.

Transformation to this new Singularity-based economy, in which the digital value chain and the social enterprise dominate, is critical as we move from the old world to the new. Companies that are not embracing emerging technologies and incorporating them into their business should be concerned. They should be worried about being shut out of the direct results of these technologies: frontier-less communities as well as the power of individuals around the globe to voice their opinions, share their expertise, and bypass traditional models for employment and business investment. If your company is not a digitally born business that is coming of age and ramping up in this new Digital Age, you will likely be falling further and further behind.

According to a recent report, the U.S. economy is only operating at 18 percent of its digital potential. The productivity gains, enabled by digital technologies, that should be showing up in the broader economy are not doing so yet—and the full potential of digitization could be worth more than $2 trillion to the economy.[1] Nearly every individual, company, and industry now has access to critical technologies designed to enhance their digital capabilities. And the early adopters are already racing ahead of the rest in terms of innovation, growth, and disruption of business models.[2] This is a final wake-up

1 James Manyika, Sree Ramaswamy, Somesh Khanna, Hugo Sarrazin, Gary Pinkus, Guru Sethupathy, and Andrew Yaffe, "Digital America: A Tale of the Haves and Have-Mores," McKinsey & Company, December 2015, https://www.mckinsey.com/industries/high-tech/our-insights/digital-america-a-tale-of-the-haves-and-have-mores.
2 Janes Manyika, Gary Pinkus, and Sree Ramaswamy, "The Most Digital Companies Are Leaving All the Rest Behind," *Harvard Business Review,* January 21, 2016, https://hbr.org/2016/01/the-most-digital-companies-are-leaving-all-the-rest-behind.